D1071385

Sustainable Consumption

Sustainable Consumption:

The Implications of Changing Infrastructures of Provision

Edited by

Dale Southerton
University of Manchester, UK

Heather Chappells
Lancaster University, UK

Bas Van Vliet
Wageningen University, The Netherlands

Edward Elgar
Cheltenham, UK • Northampton, MA, USA

Published by
Edward Elgar Publishing Limited
Glensanda House
Montpellier Parade
Cheltenham
Glos GL50 1UA
UK

Edward Elgar Publishing, Inc.
136 West Street
Suite 202
Northampton
Massachusetts 01060
USA

A catalogue record for this book
is available from the British Library

ISBN 1 84376 330 3

Printed and bound in Great Britain by MPG Books Ltd, Bodmin, Cornwall

Contents

Figures

Contributors

Noel Cass is a Research Associate at the Centre for the Study of Environmental Change, within the Institute for Environment, Philosophy and Public Policy at Lancaster University. He is conducting a national public consultation on managing the radioactive wastes from the UK nuclear submarine fleet. His work arises from a project designed to explore the social exclusionary implications of congestion charges, funded by the Department for Transport. Other research interests include climate change policy, environmental policy, transport and social justice, cultural theory, new social movements and anarchism.

Heather Chappells is currently a researcher in the Sociology Department at Lancaster University. Her recently awarded PhD thesis examined the institutional and technical construction of demand in changing networks of energy and water provision, and integrated ideas from sociology, geography and science and technology studies. Heather has worked on a variety of research projects including Smart Metering and Sustainable Cities (EPSRC, 1996–97) Domestic Consumers and Utility Services (EU DGXII, 1997–2000), and Future Comforts: Reconditioning Urban Environments (ESRC, 2003–2004).

Martin Hand is a Research Associate at the Centre for Research on Innovation and Competition at the University of Manchester. His research interests concern domestic cultures of technology and consumption, the sociology of digital technology, and Internet culture and politics. He is currently working on a project entitled Sustainable Domestic Technologies: Changing Practice, Convention and Technologies. From 1 July 2004, he will be Assistant Professor in the Department of Sociology, Queen's University, Kingston, Ontario.

Simon Marvin is Professor and Co-director of the Centre for Sustainable Urban and Regional Futures, University of Salford and the United Utilities Chair of Sustainable Urban and Regional Development. Simon's work focuses on the changing relations between cities, regions and infrastructure networks, particularly with respect to the reconfiguration of water, waste, energy, telecommunications and transportation. His research is international, working with partners in France, Denmark, Sweden, Greece and the USA with support from the European Commission, the European Science Foundation and the National Science Foundation in the USA. He has undertaken consultancy and advisory work on infrastructure issues for a range of clients, including privatized utilities, local authorities, regional agencies, the Environment Agency and the OECD.

Will Medd is a Research Fellow at the Centre for Sustainable Urban and Regional Futures, University of Salford. His research focuses on the complex and changing interconnections that configure contemporary processes of governance and socio-technical systems. Currently Will is working with international partners from Germany, Denmark, Greece, Bulgaria and Hungary on an EU-funded project looking at the emergence of 'new intermediaries' in the water sector. He is also developing research exploring the governance processes involved in 'building resilience' with particular reference to the implications for city–regional relations in the UK.

Timothy Moss, who has a DPhil in urban history, is Head of the research department Regional Institutional Change to Protect Public Goods at the Institute for Regional Development and Structural Planning (IRS) in Erkner, near Berlin. At the IRS he has coordinated and conducted a number of national and EU research projects on institutional changes affecting the provision and use of environmental resources in cities and regions. This he currently explores with regard to the transformation of technical infrastructure systems (water, energy), the institutionalization of river basin management (Water Framework Directive) and multilevel strategies for sustainable urban and regional development.

Elizabeth Shove is a Reader in Sociology at Lancaster University. Elizabeth has worked on questions of energy consumption and environmental change for a number of years and recently coordinated a European Science Foundation-funded programme of summer schools, workshops and exchanges on Consumption, Everyday Life and Sustainability. She is interested in ordinary technologies and the transformation of routines and practices and has written about *Comfort, Cleanliness and Convenience: The Social Organization of Normality* Berg (2003). She is currently working on kitchens, bathrooms and future concepts of comfort.

Dale Southerton is a Research Fellow at the ESRC Centre for Research on Innovation and Competition, University of Manchester. He specializes in the study of consumption and has previously conducted research exploring this topic in relation to identity formation, senses of belonging and distinction; the social worlds of caravanning; and the normalization of freezers. Currently he is conducting research on consumption and time-use, kitchens and bathrooms, the diffusion of cultures of consumption, and the child–parent relationship. His key research interests centre around theories of consumption, social change, innovation, sustainability, time and space, and social networks.

Gert Spaargaren is Senior Researcher and Part-time Professor on Environmental Policy for Sustainable Lifestyles and Consumption at the Environmental Policy Group of Wageningen University, the Netherlands. His main research interests and publications are in the field of environmental sociology, sustainable consumption and behaviour, and the globalization of environmental reform.

Jane Summerton is joint Professor at the Department of Technology and Social Change, and the Swedish National Road and Transport Research Institute at Linköping University. She has broad research interests within science and technology studies, particularly critical analysis of technoscientific practice, constructivist studies of risk and safety, and analysis of users' roles in infrastructures. Her latest book (Ed. with Boel Berner) is *Constructing Risk and Safety in Technological Practice* (Routledge, 2003).

John Urry is Professor of Sociology and Co-director of the Centre for Mobilities Research (CeMoRe), Lancaster University. He is author or joint author of *Contested Natures* (1998), *Sociology Beyond Societies* (2000), *The Tourist Gaze*, 2nd edn (2002), *Global Complexity* (2003) and *Performing Tourist Places* (2004). He was Chair of the UK Research Assessment Exercise Sociology Panel 1996 and 2001, and is Founding Academician, Academy of the Social Sciences.

Bas Van Vliet is Lecturer and Researcher at the Environmental Policy Group of Wageningen University, the Netherlands. His main topics of research and education are energy, water and waste infrastructures and sustainable technology development. His PhD thesis (2002) dealt with the ecological modernization of water and electricity systems, drawing upon an EU-funded research project (Domus) on domestic consumption and utility services in the UK, Sweden and the Netherlands (1997–2000).

Alan Warde is Professor of Sociology and Co-director of the ESRC Centre for Research on Innovation and Competition at the University of Manchester.

One of his main research interests is the sociology of consumption, often in relation to food. He is the author of *Consumption, Food and Taste* (Sage, 1997) and (with Lydia Martens) *Eating Out: Social Differentiation, Consumption and Pleasure* (Cambridge University Press, 2000). He is currently working on several empirical projects including a study of the diffusion of cultures of consumption, a comparative European study of trust in food, a study of cultural capital and social exclusion in the UK, and a study of kitchens and bathrooms and their relevance for issues of sustainable consumption.

Acknowledgements

We would like to thank the European Science Foundation (ESF) for its financial support of the Consumption, Everyday Life and Sustainability series of workshops and summer schools (1997–2001) and, in 2000, its funding of the Infrastructures of Consumption and the Environment workshop. Both initiatives were funded under the ESF TERM II (Tackling Environmental Resource Management) programme. We are indebted to Elizabeth Shove, Gert Spaargaren, Mika Pantzar and Hal Wilhite, who together formed the Consumption, Everyday Life and Sustainability programme steering group. Elizabeth has been of invaluable and unswerving support throughout the process of book production, and her intellectual input and friendship have been greatly valued. Thanks also to Pirkko Kasanen and Rolf Wüstenhagen who co-organized the Infrastructures of Consumption and the Environment workshop, and for Rolf's superb coordination of a meeting with the editors in St Gallen, Switzerland. Aad Correljé has provided support and ideas throughout and has made an important contribution to the shaping of this edited collection. Finally, we are grateful to all participants who contributed so much to the events listed above.

As with all books, a host of people behind the scenes deserve our unreserved gratitude. We would like to thank Joyce Wilson for her painstaking work in the editing and preparation of this book. Kerry, Charlie, Max and Isobel Southerton have all played a crucial role in keeping at least one of the editors on his toes and provided the appropriate motivation to plough ahead with the book. Trevor Dummer has been of endless support to another of the editors. Finally, Maaike Breedveld, Noor Van Vliet and the imminent arrival of another Breedveld have provided much encouragement and (welcome) distractions.

1. Introduction: consumption, infrastructures and environmental sustainability

Dale Southerton, Bas Van Vliet and Heather Chappells

The chapters in this volume originate from the Infrastructures of Consumption and the Environment workshop, held at Wageningen University, the Netherlands in 2000. The workshop built upon two international research collaborations: the European Science Foundation-funded Consumption, Everyday Life and Sustainability programme, and the European Union-funded Domus Project (Domestic Consumers and Utility Services). This volume and the initiatives from which it stemmed offer a distinctive, interdisciplinary interpretation of the issues shaping consumption that moves beyond individualistic approaches. Rather than viewing sustainable consumption as a matter of personal 'choice' or changing 'lifestyles', the emphasis is on how routine practices and consumption 'choices' are mediated through the social institutions and technical infrastructures through which services are provided.

By way of introduction, this chapter offers an overview of the issues and challenges at stake in the conceptualization and achievement of sustainable consumption. First, it describes how sustainable consumption has emerged as a key facet of environmental policy in recent years and examines how the relationship between consumption and sustainability has been understood within this context. We then consider how much of this existing material reflects a distinctly individualistic and resource-based conceptualization of what might constitute sustainable consumption. In reflecting on theories of consumption from across the social sciences, we further unravel the limitations of such an approach and reveal the value of more structural understandings of the organization of systems of consumption and provision. To demonstrate the relevance of such an approach, we concentrate on those aspects of consumption associated with infrastructure-based goods and services. We suggest that the rapid pace of infrastructure change, the environmental significance of the commodities at stake and the specific character of consumption patterns and practices, demand a reorientation of existing research and policy agendas.

SUSTAINABLE CONSUMPTION: AN EMERGENT AGENDA

Environmental research and policy have traditionally been rather one-sided, focusing primarily on how to transform production through pollution control and eco-efficiency, rather than on consumption (Organization for Economic Co-operation and Development – OECD, 2002). This imbalance is now being redressed, with sustainable consumption emerging as a key concern within national and international environmental policy agendas.

In environmental terms it is easy to see why interest in consumption has grown. Current patterns of consumption contribute to escalating CO_2 emissions and processes of global warming, as well as to increasing levels of pollution, loss of biodiversity and the depletion of finite resources. Within this highly charged context, it is not surprising that environmentalists have concentrated rather anxiously on the consumption of key resources like energy and water, on raw materials, and on the production of waste. The Brundtland report (1987) captures these concerns in its widely quoted definition of sustainable consumption:

> The use of goods and services that respond to basic needs and bring a better quality of life while minimising the use of natural resources, toxic materials and emissions of waste and pollutants over the life cycle, so as not to jeopardise the needs of future generations.

This reorientation of national and international environmental agendas towards the broad issue of sustainable consumption is further reflected in a range of recent research documents and policy publications (OECD, 2002; DEFRA, 2003; Levett et al., 2003). An examination of this material reveals a quite distinctive approach to how consumption is perceived and represented and how this frames particular sorts of strategies for sustainable provision.

One contribution is the OECD's *Towards Sustainable Household Consumption*, which offers a comprehensive evaluation of recent household consumption patterns and drivers and describes associated environmental impacts (OECD, 2002). It argues that negative environmental impacts from household activities have increased since the 1970s and forecasts an intensification of these impacts over the next 20 years, especially in areas such as energy, transport, water and waste. Particularly worrying trends are the rise in individual car use, the growth in household waste, increasing energy demand and regional imbalances in water availability.

Taking this document as an exemplar of modern policy approaches, it appears that contemporary understandings of what constitutes consumption have evolved considerably from classic economic definitions. This can be seen in a number of respects. First, consumption is defined not only in relation to market choice but also in terms of a set of choices, including the 'selection, purchase, use, maintenance, repair and disposal of any product or service' (OECD, 2002, p. 16; after Campbell, 1998). Second, it is argued that consumption is not only relevant to market valued commodities but might equally apply to non-marketed goods and services and systems of informal exchange.

Such evidence suggests that definitions of consumption have been broadened and enlarged within the mainstream environmental policy community. However, we would argue that consumption in this model is still strongly rooted in an individualistic paradigm, in that the drivers and mechanisms involved are seen to boil down to a matter of individual choice. This is apparent if we consider the representation of the key driving forces behind current and projected household consumption patterns within the OECD report. Amongst those drivers identified are rising per capita income levels that have enabled people to purchase more products and appliances; changing demographics, such as more single-person households; and changing lifestyles which have supported more individualized buying patterns (OECD, 2002, p. 12).

All of these drivers suggest that patterns of unsustainable consumption are related almost entirely to the social and economic decisions of individual households. The explicit objective for environmental researchers and policy-makers is thus translated into one of finding out which sorts of 'instruments' might lead consumers to behave in more sustainable ways or to make more pro-environmental consumption choices that involve less environmentally damaging products or services (OECD, 2002, p. 15).

Following this line of thinking, the policy challenge is interpreted as one of overcoming market or informational barriers to improved choice. In terms of the former, this has supported calls for government-led measures to restructure energy or water pricing systems, such that the environmental costs of consumption are reflected in the price of resources. In respect of the latter approach, the OECD considers the social instruments of information provision and participatory decision-making as two critical strategies for promoting sustainable consumption. It is argued that consumers need to be provided with a more consistent set of signals about their consumption patterns and associated environmental impacts across the product chain – the so-called lifecycle approach. The idea of measuring and comparing 'ecological footprints' is also rooted in this tradition (Wackernagel and Rees, 1995). The need for information-based instruments designed to change consumer behaviour, including eco-labelling or eco-efficiency campaigns, is another widely championed approach (Menanteau, 1997; Ekins, 2003).

This orientation of policy initiatives towards changing the behaviour of individual consumers is underpinned by a distinctly resource-based approach to the interpretation and analysis of sustainable consumption. By quantifying the resource impacts associated with the use of particular appliances, the individual or household becomes the basic unit of analysis. Armed with data of this type concerning the resource savings that might be made if more households changed their consumption habits, the logical step is to focus policy initiatives at the individual level in an attempt to influence the aggregated effects of individual choices. In pinning down sustainable or unsustainable consumption patterns in this way, issues such as how to reduce material intensities – for example by factors of four or ten – dominate (Noorman and Uiterkamp, 1998; Von Weizsäcker et al., 1998). Such narratives are internally consistent: they offer ways of thinking about the 'metabolism' of society and of tracing the ecological impacts of production and consumption from cradle to grave. However, as the contributions to this volume demonstrate, preoccupation with the consequences of consumption has led to a particularly restricted view of the processes through which consumption is constructed and evolves.

The sustainability agenda as currently represented by environmental researchers and policy-makers also employs a specific interpretation of technologies as 'enablers' or 'constrainers' of individual behaviour. In many eco-efficiency schemes, such as the UK's Energy Efficiency Standards of Performance (EESOP) programme, energy-saving technologies are regarded as 'fixes' that enable people to do more for less. This offers a particularly restricted and mechanistic view of how technologies shape consumption, and fails to explore how technologies and technological systems can embody certain service expectations and reproduce patterns of resource use (Shove, 2003).

The limitations of the emergent agenda for sustainable consumption can be summarized under four themes. First, deliberate efforts to reveal the environmental implications of individual action position the problem of sustainability as a problem of personal choice. The underlying assumption is that people could and would act differently if only they knew what damage they were doing. Such ideas inform programmes of research into the relationship between environmental belief and action, and the design of policy initiatives geared around the provision of more and better information. As well as embodying an arguably suspect theory of choice, exercises like this fail to appreciate the socially situated and socially structured character of consumption.

Second, much environmental policy research has tended to focus on resource-based evaluations of consumption, on aggregated individual demand and the use of homogeneous bundles of goods. Such approaches fail to recognize that consumers do not consume resources, they consume the services those resources make possible. In buying electricity, consumers are really buying lighting, heating, comfort, convenience and more. Although influential, the language of resources bears little relation to the world of consumer practice and is of limited value in understanding what people do and why.

Third, in focusing rather one-sidedly on the end-consumer, such approaches obscure important questions about the production and manufacturing of options and the intersection between design, demand and use. In practice, relationships between consumers and producers are varied and complex. Sometimes they are so varied and so complex that the distinction between them makes little sense at all.

Finally, reports like those produced by the OECD explicitly focus on environmentally sustainable consumption rather than on socially sustainable aspects of consumption, including equity or distributional effects. In this sense, environmental and social dimensions are conceptually closed off and regarded as separate spheres of interest. However, in reality, and as many of the contributions to this volume will show, such distinctions between the social worlds of people and their environments are rarely so clear-cut.

In identifying these limitations of current policy approaches, this volume advances a different sort of agenda for understanding sustainable consumption, one based on an appreciation of the social and socio-technical organization of consumption. To help identify the sorts of themes and issues that might inform such an approach, it is necessary to expand the interdisciplinary focus and seek out other ways of thinking about what is at stake in sustainable consumption.

SUSTAINABLE CONSUMPTION: REDEFINING THE AGENDA

The big questions confronting the sustainable consumption agenda have to do with definitions of well-being (Jacobs, 1995), with how societal expectations of normality are established (Shove, 2003), and with the design, construction and institutionalization of demand (Redclift, 1996; Strasser, 1999). Redefining the agenda in this way has the dual effect of connecting the study of environmental consumption with that of consumption in general, and of springing open a new toolbox of analytical and theoretical resources. Historians, anthropologists, economists, geographers, sociologists, psychologists and political economists all have things to say about the social organization of consumption and the dynamics of everyday life.

Traditionally consumption has been conceptualized in relation to the properties or values of goods and services. Utility value focuses on the application and use of goods and services in daily life (Slater, 1997). What constitutes utility value shifts according to broader sociocultural changes, as illustrated by the microwave whose utility value in the UK during the 1990s increased with the emergence of convenience foods as an important part of household food provisioning (Warde, 1999). Utility also has an influence on exchange value for the simple reason that the usefulness of a good or service impacts on what people are prepared to exchange in order to acquire that product. However, exchange value is determined by many factors beyond utility. Hirsch (1977) uses the term 'positional good' to describe objects whose exchange value is increased by the status they confer on their owners – prestige cars, antiques and works of art being prime examples. Positional goods increase exchange value because they carry symbolic value, and it is the capacities of goods and services to mediate meaning and representations of personal and social identity which make consumption such an important aspect of social life.

Considering the value of goods and services offers important conceptual building blocks for thinking about consumption. However, it does tend to focus attention on goods and services mainly provided through the market. Perhaps with the exception of some aspects of symbolic value, it also presents a rather calculative view of the processes of consuming. Writers such as Kopytoff (1986), McCracken (1986) and Miller (1987) highlight the rituals and emotions that individuals, families and social groups invest when transforming commodified goods into meaningful cultural objects. The important point is that consumption is an active process which transforms the meanings and values of goods and services and cannot be reduced simply to the properties of products as defined at the point of purchase.

It is also clear that to fully understand consumption as a process it is necessary to extend analysis beyond consuming *per se* and consider the conditioning effects of production. Economics and innovation studies highlight 'pathways of dependency' (Arthur, 1994). The cost of production, estimates of market size and expected return on investments represent critical aspects of the calculations firms make when deciding whether to provide any good or service. Crucial to such calculations is the current nature of the organization and its technologies. In other words past decisions and developments shape avenues for present and future decisions about the provisioning of goods and services.

The concept of pathways of dependency shares certain similarities with the idea of technological 'lock-in', whereby daily practices, suites of technologies and systems of provision become locked together in particular ways. Take for example the integration of the freezer, microwave, supermarkets and frozen food provisioning infrastructure, which together lock people into stable ways of ordering daily eating habits (Shove and Southerton, 2000). As well as further demonstrating the interdependencies between production and consumption, the idea of 'lock-in' highlights the role of technologies in shaping how people go about daily practices. Akrich (1992) describes how objects 'script' action, for example 'sleeping policemen' in roads forcing car drivers to slow down (Latour, 1992). Together, path-dependency, lock-in and scripts all point to the way that processes of consuming are configured by many aspects of production which have a structuring effect on what goods and services are provisioned, how those goods and services shape the consumption of related products, and how objects are used.

Mode of provision	Access/social relations	Manner of delivery	Experiences of consumption
Market	Price/exchange	Managerial	Customer/consumer
State	Need/right	Professional	Citizen/client
Household	Family/obligation	Family	Self/family/kinship
Communal	Network/reciprocity	Volunteer	Friend/neighbour/acquaintance

Source: Warde (1990).

Figure 1.1 Cycles of production and consumption

The multifaceted relationships between production and consumption are captured in Figure 1.1, which shows the many processes that accompany different modes of provision and the resulting experiences of consumption. Importantly, it highlights that much consumption is not provisioned through commercial markets, and emphasizes the differentiation between cycles of production and consumption. Through an appreciation of these interrelationships it is possible to understand not only how production configures consumption, but also how consumption configures production. For example whether water is regarded as a right for all citizens will affect the expectations and demands regarding its mode of provision.

As we have shown, consumption is not only an outcome of personal attitudes and intentions or connected with the fulfilment of utilitarian needs, but is related to the changing social, economic and technical organization of everyday life. In going beyond analyses of the behaviour of individual 'green' consumers, this volume moves toward more structural understandings of how sustainable consumption is organized. The issues and themes addressed in this edited collection are designed to emphasize the interrelatedness of systems of production and consumption and to recognize that different systems and modes of provision are an important influence on the experience of consumption (Warde, 1990; Fine and Leopold, 1993). The organization of infrastructures of provision, including water networks, energy grids, sanitation services and transportation systems are exemplars of the advantages of developing this more structural approach to the sustainable consumption agenda.

CHANGING INFRASTRUCTURES OF PROVISION AND CONSUMPTION

Utility infrastructure reconfiguration is the broad term we adopt for changes in utility infrastructures that are the result of institutional or environmental pressures. Reconfiguration may include the privatization of utility companies and the liberalization of utility markets; diversification and commodification of products and services; the splintering of formerly unified networks of provision; or the appliance of tailor-made, client-oriented technical solutions where previously uniform, large-scale technology was the standard. The possible implications of these reconfiguration processes are both far-reaching and diverse. Electricity systems might be transformed from large technical networks with a hierarchy of large-scale generation, transmission, distribution and consumption-related operations into smaller subsystems that are interconnected through a mains grid or stand-alone. Alternatively, some systems may integrate to form even more centralized systems, as in the case of waste sectors becoming dominated by incineration facilities that now face international competition.

With changing infrastructure arrangements emerging across Europe, relationships between consumers and providers in the utilities sectors are no longer self-evidently based on the premises of public service provision. Providers may try to compete for those consumers they view as the most profitable, while consumers in remote areas may find it more worthwhile to seek forms of self-provision, taking themselves off conventional grids. On the other hand, providers of utility services might attempt to take consumer demands more seriously than before as they struggle to find (or construct) niche markets for a diverse range of services.

In examining these dynamics, the book will reconsider the arguments for and against utility restructuring in relation to the development of more sustainable infrastructures of consumption. The case for market liberalization suggests that the sovereign consumer will have greater control over the provision of goods and services as a consequence of the improved consumption choices made available to them. Providing consumers are informed of the implications of such choices, and that they are motivated accordingly, it is assumed that more sustainable forms of consumption will follow. Sceptics argue that liberalization and the greater differentiation of services may act to reinforce less sustainable forms of consumption, especially if they reduce the economic costs of goods and services which are the least environmentally friendly at the expense of those which are more so. Our intention in this volume is to re-examine and extend these arguments and to show how relationships between consumption, provision and sustainability are rarely so clear-cut.

CHAPTERS AND CONTENTS

The book is organized around three themes, each of which contributes to the development of a more structural understanding of the relation between patterns of sustainable consumption and changing systems of infrastructure provision. Part I addresses the theme of consumption, lifestyle and choice and examines the conceptual application of consumption to theoretical and policy-oriented accounts of environmental sustainability.

In Chapter 2, Gert Spaargaren argues that bringing in issues of sustainable consumption and lifestyles should complement the analysis of sustainable production. It is possible to place a stronger emphasis on consumption issues without lapsing into the socio-psychological models which were used for so long in the analyses of environmental (un)friendly behaviours of citizen-consumers. The chapter argues that the social practices model, derived from structuration theory, offers a feasible alternative in this respect because the model makes possible a sociological, contextual approach to consumption behaviours and lifestyles. The questions for empirical research raised by the social practices model are illustrated using the example of domestic consumption of utility products and services. By discussing a number of pilot studies within Dutch environmental policy-making, the future agenda of the politics of sustainable consumption is explored and commented upon.

Theories of practice also feature prominently in Chapter 3. Dale Southerton, Alan Warde and Martin Hand review different conceptualizations of consumption within the sustainability agenda. They identify three types of (not mutually exclusive) accounts of consumption and four policy responses which draw on these accounts to varying extents. They argue that many of these accounts and policy responses are based on a particular conceptualization of consumption: a view of the autonomous consumer exercising relatively unconstrained lifestyle choices. This way of conceptualizing consumption has its roots in neo-classical economics and in some influential theories of late- and post-modernity. This is despite a significant theoretical and empirical body of literature which emphasizes how consumption is socially constrained and embedded within routine and normative practices of daily life. Taking the case of the emergence of showering in the UK, they argue that the conventions of any practice unfold through the continuous separation and interlocking of many practices, and it is understanding these processes that represents the challenge for the sustainable consumption agenda.

Jane Summerton further examines the conceptual value of the rhetoric of choice in relation to utility consumption in Chapter 4. Focusing on recent changes in the organization of energy provision in the UK, the USA and Scandinavia she describes the striking paradox of market liberalization: that a system which purports to offer increased choice to consumers actually limits the options available to many of these groups. She suggests that the decoupling of the environmental or the economic from the social dimensions of sustainability increases the social inequalities that surround energy provision, with the most affluent groups receiving the greater share of consumer benefits associated with market liberalization.

Part II examines how new scales of provision and intermediaries challenge assumptions regarding the organization of systems of infrastructure provision, and calls for a re-examination of the character of relationships between consumers and providers. In Chapter 5, Bas Van Vliet suggests that arguments about the relative environmental efficiency or sustainability of infrastructure systems, based purely on the dichotomous distinction between small or large-scale provision, are weakened once account is taken of the multiple dimensions of scale that now exist. In examining a variety of new modes of socio-technical organization within the Dutch water, waste and energy sectors he shows how a more sophisticated interpretation of scale and its relation to environmental performance is now required.

Chapter 6 draws attention to how new social and technical intermediaries have dissolved the conceptual space between utilities and their users, and in the process have facilitated new contexts for environmental action in between the spheres of consumption and provision. In reviewing a variety of these new intermediary arrangements in the UK water sector, Simon Marvin and Will Medd show how a radically different landscape of interaction and new opportunities for sustainable consumption is being forged.

The final theme, in Part III, is the interface between infrastructural change and inflexibility. Each of the contributions challenges the view that contemporary utility consumption can be understood in terms of largely unrestricted choices or isolated activities that are disconnected from the socio-technical infrastructure at large.

Tim Moss, in his investigation of the restructuring of water and wastewater networks in Berlin, shows how technical infrastructures cannot be uprooted overnight, and nor can the organizational legacy these embody be easily overturned. As a consequence, Chapter 7 demonstrates how some patterns of consumption become reproduced within the system, clashing with contemporary views of what is environmentally sustainable.

Transport networks are associated with mobility and movement, but in Chapter 8 Noel Cass, Elizabeth Shove and John Urry show how they also represent moments of immobility and inflexibility that reflect specific constellations of socio-technical networks and embodied notions of time and space. It is only by developing methods of analysis that appreciate the interfacing of these different socio-technical and spatial–temporal elements in specific contexts that the linkages between consumption and production, and opportunities for environmental change, can be understood.

Continuing this theme, Heather Chappells and Elizabeth Shove describe how networks feature quite specific organizational rules and modes of operation that reflect past, present and future expectations. Focusing on the actual workings of both mainstream and marginal electricity and water systems in the UK, they show how the orchestration of resources and management of demand are dependent on the ability of current supply chain managers to negotiate and configure new socio-technical interdependencies across the system as a whole.

The concluding chapter considers the pivotal themes that emerge from the contributions to this volume in terms of their relevance for understanding utility infrastructure reconfiguration, and what this means for sustainable consumption. How these themes might be enrolled to understand the social organization of sustainable consumption at large, and how such insights can be used to inform the development of a more structural and interdisciplinary research agenda on sustainable consumption, are detailed. Such an agenda requires the reframing of theoretical and policy debates in order to account for the embedded and conventionalized practices of daily life within which most acts of consumption take place, and the configuration of socio-technical systems that are organized at a range of scales and configured with different levels of flexibility.

PART I

Consumption, lifestyle and choice

2. Sustainable consumption: a theoretical and environmental policy perspective[1]

Gert Spaargaren[2]

INTRODUCTION

By bringing consumption issues to the fore, this chapter reflects the general trend to attach greater importance to the role of citizen-consumers in shaping and reproducing some of the core institutions of production and consumption. At the present time, the opinions and behaviours of citizen-consumers matter increasingly for companies, policy-makers and social movements. The shifting emphasis from production to consumption, and the concomitant weight attached to the dynamics of civil society, are expressed by stating that there has been a consumerist turn within sociology (Featherstone, 1983). This chapter makes the central argument that environmental sociologists need to conceptualize sustainable consumption behaviour, lifestyles and daily routines in such a way as to avoid the pitfalls of many of the so-called micro-approaches that have been developed to date. It argues for a contextual approach to sustainable consumption and for that purpose try to develop a conceptual model which combines a focus on the central role of human agency with proper treatment of the equally important role of social structure. Structuration theory as developed by Anthony Giddens (1984, 1991a) provides the conceptual key to a solution of the classical actor–structure dilemma by putting forward social practices as the proper unit of analysis for researchers and policy-makers. The social practices model is used, first to analyse the process of diffusion of environmental innovations in utility sectors, and secondly to discuss the emergence of a variety of lifestyles or lifestyle groups in the field of the sustainable consumption of energy, water and waste services. In section 3 the general policy discourse on consumer-oriented environmental politics is discussed and evaluated in light of relevant policy experiments in the field of sustainable consumption in the Netherlands. Such a review is necessary in order to develop the future agenda for research and policy-making on sustainable consumption. In conclusion it is argued that an international network of social scientists working in the field of sustainable consumption can help significantly in developing a comparative perspective to sustainable consumption in a globalizing world.

A CONTEXTUAL APPROACH TO CONSUMPTION: THE SOCIAL PRACTICES MODEL

After a long period of abstract criticisms on consumer culture, general sociology has now taken up the study of consumption in a serious way. Despite this, pride of place within the emerging sociology of consumption (Warde, 1990; Otnes, 1988) has not yet been given to environmental issues. The first edited volume on sustainable consumption in this field was issued only recently (Cohen and Murphy, 2001).

Within environmental sociology, the study of consumption behaviour and lifestyles has for a long time been the domain of empirical researchers who in many cases are theoretically inspired by a variant of the social psychological model of human behaviour (Fishbein and Atzjen, 1975). When applied within the field of environmental studies,[3] this so-called Attitude–Behaviour model uses the individual attitude or norm to predict the concrete future behaviour of individuals. This behaviour is conceived of in terms of a great number of separate items or issues that are used as indicators for a more encompassing environmental consciousness or awareness. Among the symbolic representations of a high environmental consciousness and the corresponding environmentally correct behaviours were the intended use of non-phosphate detergents; the promise of avoiding throwaway plastic bags and packages while shopping; and the tendency to use bicycles instead of cars for short-distance mobility.

The sociological model as presented in Figure 2.1 differs from the socio-psychological Attitude–Behaviour model in some crucial respects. Firstly, at the centre of the model one finds not the individual attitude or norm but rather the actual behavioural practices, situated in time and space, which an individual shares with other human agents. Secondly, the model does not focus on specific, isolated behavioural items but looks into the possibilities for designated groups of actors to reduce the overall environmental impacts of their normal daily routines involving clothing, food, shelter, travel, sport and leisure. Thirdly, the model analyses the process of reducing the environmental impacts of consumption in distinct domains of social life in terms of the deliberate achievements of knowledgeable and capable agents who make use of the possibilities offered to them in the context of specific systems of provision. By adding this focus on systems of provision (Fine and Leopold, 1993; Shove, 1997; Shove and Chappells, 1999), social structures are no longer treated as external variables but are brought into the centre of the analysis.

ACTOR/AGENT - -HUMAN ACTION - - SOCIAL PRACTICES - - - - - -STRUCTURES

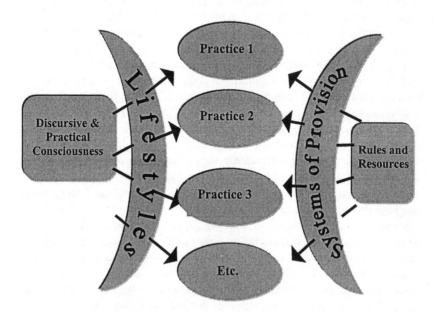

Figure 2.1 Social practices and the duality of structure

By replacing the Attitude–Behaviour model with the social practices model as the central framework for analyses, critical changes emerge with regard to the conceptual foci of environmental research and policy-making. The sections below briefly discuss three consequences of working with this model.

The End of the Individual as the (Only) Relevant Unit of Analysis

First, the social practices model implies the end of the individual as the central unit of analysis. Human agency is analysed not in terms of the isolated individual or the 'homo clausus' (Elias, 1971) but rather in terms of the twin concepts of lifestyles and social practices. The lifestyle of each individual is constructed from a series of building-block corresponding to the set of social practices an individual invokes when pursuing his or her daily life. The lifestyle of an individual human agent is defined by Giddens as the set of social practices which an individual embraces, together with the storytelling that goes along with it (Giddens, 1991a, p. 81). When interpreted in this way, it becomes clear that the concept of a 'green' or sustainable lifestyle is different from the concept of an environmentally friendly attitude since it cannot be measured using only one dimension or scale.[4] Green lifestyles are composed of lifestyle segments or sectors which may vary considerably among themselves with respect to the contribution they make to the net environmental impact of the lifestyle of the individual human agent. Even individuals who state the intention to follow strictly and frequently environmental criteria that form the foundational principles of their lifestyle will act against these intentions certain times and under particular circumstances in some segments of their lifestyle. Furthermore, some people deliberately insulate specific practices or lifestyle segments from the environmental considerations they accept and apply as legitimate rules most of the time and in most other segments of their lifestyles. In Dutch environmental discourse this mechanism is recognized and has come to be represented by the image of a typical Harley-Davidson motorcyclist who also proves to be an active member of a so-called Eco-team or GAP-team[5] in his neighbourhood. This image is used in information campaigns by environmental policy-makers to illustrate the fact that a person does not have to be written off for climate change politics once he or she apparently acts against the established rules for sustainable behaviour in one or two domains of daily life (VROM, 2000). The probably considerable CO_2 emissions of the Harley-Davidson can for example be compensated for by a set of rather strict energy policies applied in the domain of domestic consumption.

Environmental Policy Goals to be Defined from a Life-world Perspective

A second consequence of working with the social practices model is the need to reformulate most of the existing targets in environmental policy-making. Within the present policy framework, the central aims are formulated in an exclusively technical language, addressed mainly to institutional actors in the sphere of industrial production. When daily routines like clothing, food, shelter, travel, sport and leisure are taken as a starting point for policy-making, these policy definitions must be reformulated and specified from a life-world perspective in order to be recognized and taken on board by concrete (lifestyle) groups of citizen-consumers.

Key actors in Dutch environmental policy circles are taking up the challenge to develop sets of environmental indicators for all major social practices. So far these sets of indicators continue to rely on the technical rationale so prominent in environmental policy-making.[6]

In order to make the policy targets in the different social practices or consumption domains recognizable and perceptible for citizen-consumers, the indicators have to be reformatted according to the rationale of the life-world itself. Only when a social dimension is added to the technical criteria will citizen-consumers, in the context of enacting their daily routines, be able to arrive quickly, correctly and routinely at the position in which they know about the relevant environmental aspects of their routines. To help them accomplish this, we would argue for the need to develop so-called 'environmental heuristics' for each social practice. Environmental heuristics can be regarded as rules-of-thumb to be used by citizen-consumers in determining 'how to go on' in a more sustainable way in the context of the time–space-bound daily routines in which they are involved. These heuristics connect the predominantly technical rationale of environmentalism to the social rationale of the life-world and at the same time reduce the complexity of sustainable consumption in such a way that it fits the practical logic of daily life. Some examples of more or less well-known heuristics are the principle of waste prevention and separation ('keep them apart'), the use of eco-labels ('buy green') and the use of the modal-shift notion in transport ('park and ride').

Contextualizing Individual Responsibility for Environmental Change

The third consequence has to do with the issue of individual responsibility for environmental social change. In the social practices approach, the responsibility of the individual towards environmental change is analysed in direct relation with social structure. The individual possibilities and the disposition of the individual towards environmental social change are analysed in conjunction with the levels and modes of green provisioning. When there is a high level – both in quantitative and qualitative respects – of green provisioning, people are more or less brought into a position in which the greening of their corresponding lifestyle segment becomes a feasible option. By emphasizing the role of systems of provision, the enabling aspects of social structure are emphasized.

In the case of the Netherlands, it is obvious that within some social practices the levels of green provisioning are much higher than in the case of others. This is due to the fact that the ecological modernization of production and consumption does not develop at the same pace and in the same way through the different sectors of production and the corresponding systems of provision. For example, in many European countries there are considerably more green options available in the food chain (Schuttelaar & Partners, 2000) as compared to the travel industry (Bargeman, 2001; Beckers et al., 2000).

If we contextualize the norms and environmental behaviours of individual human actors, we not only move away from overly individualistic accounts of environmental change, but at the same time open up a new research agenda for environmental sociology through the study of environmental change from a life-world perspective. Some elements of this new research agenda will be discussed in the next section.

SUSTAINABLE CONSUMPTION IN CONTEXT: THE EXAMPLE OF UTILITY PROVISION

The fact that levels of provisioning for sustainable alternatives differ among social practices is well recognized within the environmental sciences. The kind of choices made available to citizen-consumers, in addition to the classical properties like quality and prices of products and services, have also been investigated to a considerable extent (Vringer and Blok, 1993; Blok and Vringer, 1995). Much less attention has been paid to the social conditions and circumstances which frame green or sustainable alternatives. Environmental sociologists can make a vital contribution on this point by investigating the social relations which go together with the socio-technical innovations implied in the ecological modernization of consumption. It must be clarified whether, on the one hand, the greening of social practices like feeding or dwelling makes citizen-consumers more dependent on expert systems which are hard to access and impossible to control, or, on the other hand, whether sustainable versions enhance the authority of consumers, who are thereby able to exert democratic control over the major actors involved in providing green alternatives.[7]

The changing context for sustainable consumption, and more specifically the changing social relations between providers and citizen-consumers, formed the central questions for the Domus research project (1997–2000) which was funded by the European Union and conducted by an international team of researchers from the UK, Sweden and the Netherlands, using a comparative research methodology (Chappells et al., 2000; Van Vliet et al., 2000; Raman et al., 2000). A brief discussion of the theoretical and empirical aspects of this research project will help elucidate the ways in which social context can be given a proper place in the analyses of sustainable consumption.

An Infrastructural and Historical Perspective

When the social practice of inhabiting a house is taken as a starting point, the possibilities for householders to green their consumption can be said to be determined to a large extent by the green alternatives made available in the fields of energy, water and waste. The Domus team investigated the kind of green alternatives which some of the major providers in different European countries had endorsed from about the mid-1980s onwards. To analyse the packages of green alternatives offered by the providers of energy, water and waste services, the system of provision perspective, also referred to as the 'infrastructural perspective', was used as an analytical tool. Within this infrastructural perspective, special emphasis is placed on the ways in which modes of design, production and distribution at the provider end of the chain do, or do not, correspond with certain modes of access, use and disposal at the consumer end of the chain.

From the empirical research it became evident first that power relations between providers and consumers are multi-sided phenomena and second that these relations go through a rapid and rather profound process of change. To make sense of this variety and to establish the overall direction of the changes involved, a historical perspective had to be introduced.

In Europe, the process of householders 'serving and being served' (Otnes, 1988) by utility-like organizations was rather predictable and one dimensional during the Fordist period between the 1950s and 1970s. In most European countries, householders were connected to networks that were most of the time monopolistic in nature and controlled by national governments. Householders had no choice other than buying – at a fixed tariff – the commodities and services they needed in order to be able to sustain their domestic social life. Today by contrast we witness major, long-term changes in utility provision, changes that will alter the very nature of the provision–consumption process and which are comparable to the kind of changes Ruth Schwartz-Cowan analysed in her impressive book *More Work for Mother* (1983). While Schwartz-Cowan describes the ways in which the industrialization of households in the USA resulted in a new set of power relations and technical interdependencies between networks of utility providers and householders, we are now witnessing the dissolution of this 'modern' form of serving and being served which is being replaced by a late-modern variation of utility provisioning.

In the late-modern condition of the global network society we must, as Guy and Marvin argue (Guy and Marvin, 1996; Guy et al., 1997, 2001), analyse the provision and consumption of utility goods and services against a background of splintering, fragmented or differentiating networks, linking providers and consumers in many different ways. Figure 2.2 presents a very simplified representation of the pre-modern, modern and late-modern configurations in utility service provision and consumption, also illustrating the different positions of householders vis-à-vis provider networks.

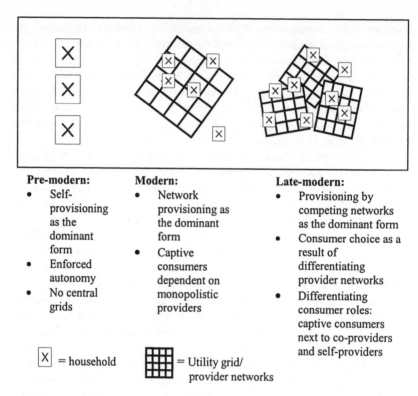

Pre-modern:
- Self-provisioning as the dominant form
- Enforced autonomy
- No central grids

Modern:
- Network provisioning as the dominant form
- Captive consumers dependent on monopolistic providers

Late-modern:
- Provisioning by competing networks as the dominant form
- Consumer choice as a result of differentiating provider networks
- Differentiating consumer roles: captive consumers next to co-providers and self-providers

$\boxed{X}$ = household   ▦ = Utility grid/ provider networks

Figure 2.2 Pre-modern, modern and late-modern forms of utility provision and consumption

The Social Dimension of Environmental Innovation

With the help of the infrastructural and historical perspective, it could first be established that in the field of domestic consumption of water, energy and waste services, a substantial number of innovations were introduced under the heading of sustainability in several European countries from the mid-1980s onward.[8] Second, Domus researchers demonstrated that these socio-technical innovations varied considerably in terms of their associated social relations. When combining both results, one can conclude that the ecological modernization within networks of utility provision is to a great extent carried by and dependent on technological innovations, but these innovations are socially variable in that social relations are not determined by sustainable technologies. Perhaps this may sound obvious to sociologists, but it is not so for many environmental engineers who are working in the expert systems involved in the renewal of utility provision. The box below, which discusses green electricity provision with the help of photovoltaic (PV) cell technology, provides a useful example.

PV TECHNOLOGY IN THE BUILT ENVIRONMENT: TWO CASE STUDIES

PV solar panels are among the most widely recognized and used symbolic representations of sustainable energy provision and consumption in the Netherlands, and over the past ten years the application and integration of PV technology in the built environment have become one of the main goals of energy policies. However, the ways in which the PV panels are integrated in living areas, and especially the social conditions of their application and use, are very different.

In the Amsterdam area, there has been a major pilot project for the large-scale integration of PV panels in the built environment by roofing hundreds of family dwellings[9] with them. The panels are owned by the utility company and the electricity generated is plugged directly into the central electricity grid, without the householders knowing about the actual energy performance of the panels, let alone that they were able to use the green electricity generated on the roof of their own dwelling. In short, householders were not regarded as – nor offered the possibility to become – functional stakeholders (www.zon-pv.nl).

It was possible to compare this situation with a technically identical situation in the eastern part of the country, where the municipalities of Amersfoort and Apeldoorn decided to work together with the (privatized) utility companies to offer, on the basis of attractive financial conditions, PV roofs to citizens who had just bought a house in a newly built area. Citizen-consumers could either rent or buy the PV-panelled roof from the utility company. There was also a double metering system installed, monitoring both the self-produced solar energy and the amount of energy which householders bought from or redelivered to the central grid, this grid functioning as a back-up system for the domestic PV systems. One can expect the commitment citizen-consumers in Amersfoort and Apeldoorn will develop with respect to their 'own', visible, servicing PV system to be qualitatively and quantitatively different when compared to the Amsterdam situation. Yet from the outside the dwellings look identical.

From this and many similar empirical cases we were able to conclude that the social relations which accompany the application of sustainable technologies at the domestic level show remarkable and relevant differences which cannot be explained by, or reduced to, differences in the technologies themselves (Spaargaren, 2000).[10] As a consequence we conclude that the greening of domestic consumption cannot be properly understood by looking into the technology in an isolated way. The development, diffusion and application of sustainable technical devices must be analysed against the background of the broader societal dynamics in utility provisioning and consumption (Van Vliet, 2002). Environmental innovations are shaped by the forces of liberalization and privatization, but also contribute to these developments in a specific way.

Liberalization, Privatization and the Emergence of 'Green Choices'

Although the pace of change will be different in different sectors and societies,[11] the general direction of change within the European Union is clear. In Europe there is a process of differentiation of utility provision and consumption evolving, which seems to have no precedent in history. This process of differentiation implies that more options are offered to citizen-consumers in these sectors than before. Green options are emerging first and foremost with respect to the resource base of domestic energy provision, the quality and/or reusability of domestic drinking water, the nature of domestic sewage systems, and the schemes for handling domestic solid waste. This differentiation in the resource base (Rs) of domestic consumption is displayed in the column on the right-hand side of Figure 2.3. However, the process of differentiation does not halt here. Differentiation pertains to the social or power relations between providers and citizen-consumers as well. Due to the liberalization of electricity markets, citizen-consumers are given the choice to select their own provider and also to have a say in the social conditions surrounding the provision of domestic utility services. In the Netherlands the case of green electricity schemes serves as an example, especially given that Dutch householders have been free to choose their provider of green electricity since July 2001. With the liberation of formerly captive consumers, a process is set in motion in which providers have to compete for end-users, including households. In the context of this competition, green products, services and strategies start to be taken on as strategic resources by utility companies. The differentiation between providers (P) and with respect to provider–consumer relations is expressed in the middle column of Figure 2.3.

The most interesting aspect of the differentiation process however is to be found in the left-hand column of Figure 2.3. Here it is envisaged that due to

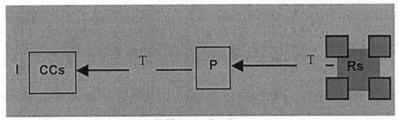

Step 1: resource differentiation

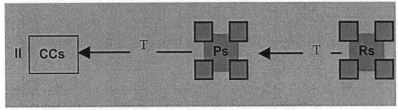

Step 2: (also) providers – differentiation

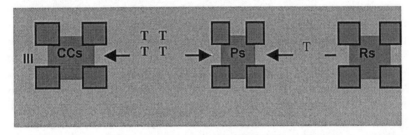

Step 3: (also) consumers – differentiation

[CCs = consumers, Ps = providers, Rs = resources and T = (monitoring) technologies]

Figure 2.3 Dimensions of differentiation in utility provision (based on Van Vliet, 2002 and Chappells et al., 2000)

the differentiation process in utility provision, in the end there will also emerge different lifestyle groups of citizen-consumers (CCs). These lifestyle groups are differentiated by the different ways in which they engage themselves with sustainable utility consumption and (co-)provision. Some providers – both companies and governments – begin to recognize this process and start to make use of lifestyle and distinction aspects to promote more sustainable patterns of domestic consumption.[12] In Sweden for example one electricity company contributed to the lifestyle patterning of householders by introducing different colours, not for the different resource bases themselves but for different lifestyle groups of citizen-consumers. The red, blue, yellow or green lifestyle groups are characterized by a specific use-pattern of electricity, which to a certain extent is said to result from their lifestyles (Summerton, 2000).

In sum, we might conclude from the discussion in this section that in the European Union a process of differentiation in utility sectors can be detected which results, among other things, in more green options for distinct groups of citizen-consumers. Such choices refer not only to the technical dimension of utility provision and consumption but to the social dimension as well. Consequently, based on the dynamics of differentiation and the resulting green choices, lifestyle groups could come forward which distinguish themselves by the specific ways in which they do – or do not – make use of more sustainable alternatives to green different segments of their lifestyles.

POLICY-MAKING AND RESEARCH ON SUSTAINABLE CONSUMPTION IN THE NETHERLANDS

The (non-) handling of socio-technical innovations by emerging lifestyle groups of citizen-consumers has the potential to become an important subject for future research and policy-making. Research should clarify when and how, and under what lifestyle conditions, different groups of citizen-consumers make use of the socio-technical innovations made available to them in the various consumption domains. At the moment the research agenda on the politics of sustainable consumption is just barely in the making, and most of the work still needs to be done. As a contribution to the debate, I will introduce and discuss three pilot projects that were recently conducted in the Netherlands in an effort to develop new consumer-oriented environmental politics aimed at reducing the environmental impacts of consumption. The pilot projects were designed and implemented in close collaboration with scientific researchers and policy-makers and were intended to deliver some essential building-blocks for consumer-oriented environmental politics in the future. Each pilot project will be evaluated using the social practices model developed in section 2, with emphasis on the kind of questions generated by this model for future research on the politics of sustainable consumption.

The 'Domain Explorations'

By conducting a number of so-called 'Domain Explorations' (*Domeinverkenningen*) researchers attempted to establish the precise environmental profile of a series of social practices judged to be relevant in the context of consumer-oriented environmental politics (Schuttelaar & Partners, 2000; CREM, 2000; TNO, 1999). Food, clothing, housing, leisure, personal care and sport were assessed with respect to their environmental impacts as well as their potential for reducing those impacts. The nature of the environmental impacts within the different consumption domains being established, the government organized in the next phase of the process a consultation with the main actors involved in the various consumption domains. For the social practice of domestic food consumption, these so-called chain-platforms, bringing together all the major actors from food-related production–consumption chains, were already organized in 2001.[13]

The innovative element of the 'Domain Explorations' refers to the effort to translate the environmental goals, as set at the national level, into a series of daily routines. However, the job of translating was only halfway completed, since the 'Domain Explorations' still hold on to the technical vocabulary which appears to be characteristic of environmental policy-making in general. In terms of the social practices model, one could conclude that the 'Domain Explorations' delivered the raw materials from which the environmental heuristics for the different consumption domains should be processed.

'Citizens and the Environment' Experiments

A second series of policy pilots, which were conducted under the label 'Citizens and the Environment' experiments (*Burger en Milieu-experimenten*), stressed the need to take into account the life-world rationality which citizen-consumers use to enact their daily consumption routines (B&A Groep, 2000). To illustrate the pressing need to evaluate environmental policy-making along these lines, researchers went out to visit shopping centres, pubs and childcare centres to observe the (environmentally relevant) behaviours of these situated groups of citizen-consumers, and to invite them to a focus-group meeting to be organized at a later time. During these meetings, which were also attended by environmental policy-makers, citizen-consumers could bring to the fore their views on the (mis)match of formal environmental policies on the one hand and the rationality of their everyday life on the other. From these 'Citizen and the Environment' experiments, it was revealed that environmental policies in general were lacking a sensitivity to the problems of everyday life, and that for most of the policy goals, most of the time, most of the citizens were not able to establish the link with everyday life by themselves.

The 'Future Perspective Project'

Assuming that the environmental goals with respect to all the relevant consumption domains (clothing, feeding, travelling and so on) are clear and also accepted by citizen-consumers, would it then actually be possible to reduce substantially the environmental impacts of daily routines in modern industrialized societies like the Netherlands? In other words, are there enough socio-technical innovations available to citizen-consumers which can be used to green their lifestyles, without the need to abandon the existing high-quality levels of modern consumption? To explore these possibilities, a third research experiment was conducted in concerted action by policy-makers and environmental researchers. In the 'Future Perspective Project' (*Project Perspectief*) a small number of householders accepted the challenge to substantially reduce, within a circumscribed period of time, the environmental impacts of their daily consumption routines. In exchange for their willingness to participate, citizen-consumers were provided with the relevant resources (money, knowledge)[14] by the government. From this research project it was learned that the possibilities for sustainable consumption are indeed different within different domains of daily consumption. Some routines are more difficult to change than others, partly because the emotions invested in them are different but, more substantively, because of the fact that the level of provisioning of green alternatives turned out to be different for the social practices distinguished.[15]

CONCLUSION

The various research and policy experiments described above help to develop the future agenda for consumer-oriented research and policy-making. The social practices model can be seen as an attempt to combine some of the essential building-blocks into an integrated strategy, emphasizing the need to:

- Establish sets of environmental heuristics for all the major social practices which can be said to be relevant for environmental policy-making. These environmental heuristics inevitably involve a mixture of the technical rationality which dominates the provider networks on the one hand, and the life-world rationalities used by citizen-consumers to organize their daily lives on the other. The 'Domain Explorations' as well as the 'Citizen and the Environment' experiments provide valuable inputs for the development of these heuristics. From the 'Citizen and the Environment' experiments it can be concluded that the consultation of circumscribed groups of citizen-consumers at different phases of the process is a prerequisite.

- Identify and analyse in some detail the actual and potential 'routes for innovation' within the selected social practices. The level of sustainable provisioning in terms of both the quantity and the quality of the sustainable alternatives offered to specific lifestyle groups of citizen-consumers must be determined. With the help of the system of provision perspective, these innovation routes can and should be specified in terms of the modes of design, production, distribution, access, use and disposal which prevail in the selected social practices or consumption domains. To understand why some socio-technical innovations are being picked up by specific groups of citizen-consumers and not others, lock-in factors or 'slots' have to be identified and analysed as they can occur at all the relevant sections of the production–consumption chains.[16]

- Provide a description and analyses of the different lifestyle groups which emerge from the stylized and symbolized use that is being made of the environmental innovations at the level of the particular social practices. This implies not only that new conceptual tools have to be developed to discuss classes or 'tribes' (Bauman, 1983) of sustainable consumers, but also that new research methodologies and forms of data collection are needed.[17]

- (Re)define the role of both governmental and non-governmental actors in consumer-oriented environmental policy-making at different levels. These roles will be different for the different social practices and also depend on the phase of the process and the tasks at hand.[18] The urge to take into account participatory forms of policy-making should be obvious in this respect.

This agenda may turn out to be overly ambitious, and it will take a considerable amount of time and research to develop it into a body of knowledge which is scientifically solid and relevant to policy-making. However, the goal of turning environmental policy-making and policy-makers towards the direction of citizen-consumers makes it worth the effort.

EPILOGUE

This analysis of sustainable consumption draws upon empirical research from European countries only, raising issues of its Eurocentric biases and the problems which can occur when applying the analysis to other parts of the global network society (Mol, 2001). For example, the greening of food practices of consumers in rich countries could very well result in new inequalities within global food chains, and eco-tourism has already been recognized for its social distributional impacts. To protect the emerging field of sustainable consumption from small-mindedness, a transnational, comparative approach must be argued for (Wilhite, 1997). The further development of international networks of researchers on sustainable consumption[19] should be welcomed in this respect.

NOTES

1. Copyright (2003) from Spaargaren (2003). Reproduced by permission of Taylor & Francis, http://www.routledge-ny.com.
2. This chapter improved considerably due to the comments of Arthur Mol, Peter Oosterveer, Anne Scheinberg and the constructive criticisms of four anonymous *Society and Natural Resources* reviewers.
3. We are aware of the fact that many authors have developed and refined the original formulation of the Attitude–Behaviour model since its first introduction, without altering however the basic assumptions on which the model rests. For a recent overview, see the discussion by Peter Ester in Beckers et al. (1999).
4. For an interesting piece of research which tries to combine both perspectives see Thøgersen and Ölander (2001).
5. Eco-teams are part of the international Global Action Plan (GAP). The eco-team brings together a small number of people interested in reducing the overall environmental impacts of their domestic consumption (Staats and Harland, 1995).
6. See also section 3 on policy-making and research on sustainable consumption in the Netherlands, where the so-called 'Domain Explorations' (*Domeinverkenningen*) are introduced and discussed.
7. The way in which the actual use of utility flows is measured or monitored illustrates the power relations involved. Metering technologies can be applied as a mode of end-user surveillance or to make transparent to the end-user the 'expert system' as it operates at the other side of the meter. See also Burg et al. (2001) and Marvin et al. (1999).
8. For a detailed description of over 150 socio-technical innovations in the three countries from the Domus project, see Raman et al. (2000).
9. In Amersfoort for example 500 houses were included, covered with 12 000 m² of PV solar panels.
10. Van Mierlo looked into the factors which could help explain the differences between the Amsterdam and the Amersfoort projects, and arrived at the conclusion that the different dynamics between the provider networks involved contributed most to the explanation (Van Mierlo, 1997).
11. Uneven developments are described in a series of national reports on the historical development of the utility sectors in Sweden, the Netherlands and the UK. For example, while the UK is a front-runner in privatization, the Netherlands and Sweden have in general a more developed environmental history in utility provision. Also in almost every country the energy sectors turn out to be ahead of the water sectors with respect to privatization. And last but not least all privatization efforts are fuelled by EU policies, along with most of the environmental measures which go along with these changes (Chappells et al., 2000).
12. The Dutch government for example agreed on liberalizing first only the green electricity schemes, while also offering relief from existing eco-taxes on domestic energy to those householders who selected such a scheme. As a result, green electricity markets are no longer regarded as insignificant niche markets, with 1 million users (total population 16 million) of green electricity one year after liberalization of the market in the Netherlands

(www.greenprice.nl) and with revenues from eco-taxes in many countries of the EU mounting from 6 to 10 per cent of total taxes. In the Netherlands eco-taxes amounted to 15 billion euros, representing 15 per cent of total tax revenues in 2001 (Bos, 2001).

13. The chain platforms were inspired by the rather successful forms of horizontal policy-making applied in the 1980s with respect to different target groups in the sphere of production. These forms of 'Joint Environmental Policy-making' (JEP) resulted in a considerable number of voluntary agreements between government and industry and were regarded as rather effective from an environmental policy-making point of view (for further information on JEP, see Mol et al., 2000).

14. Twelve families received a 10 per cent increase in income and were regularly assisted by a 'coach' who helped to organize the monitoring of environmental impacts on a daily basis, and who could also advise them about possible alternative courses of action (CEA, 1999). A software program was made available to the families to check the environmental impacts of the products they purchased.

15. The consumption patterns of participating households were again evaluated a year and a half after the formal ending of the project. It turned out that, for example, newly established routines in the area of food were judged by participants to be easier to sustain than those in the area of leisure and tourism (Rescon, 2000).

16. Environmental sociologists can profit from the work on innovation and diffusion of technology by Pinch and Bijker (1987), Schot (1992, 1998), Kemp (1994), Rotmans et al. (2001), Shove and Southerton (2000) and many others.

17. Research methodologies and data sets as developed by Socio-Consult in the context of the Bourdieu-inspired 'Motivaction project' might serve as an example here (Motivaction, 1999).

18. In Spaargaren (2001), the different phases of the process in terms of the policy cycle model as introduced in the Netherlands by Winsemius (1986) is discussed.

19. The Lancaster-based ESF network on 'Consumption, Everyday Life and the Environment' could be mentioned as an example, although less-developed countries were underrepresented.

3. The limited autonomy of the consumer: implications for sustainable consumption

Dale Southerton, Alan Warde and Martin Hand

INTRODUCTION

It is widely believed that current levels of consumption required to maintain acceptable standards of living in affluent societies are unsustainable. A host of explanations are put forward to account for such unprecedented volumes of consumption. Some point the finger at the relationship between a capitalist system of production and resource distribution, which places profit before ecological concerns (Daly, 1996). The system must reproduce itself by selling ever more goods and services in order that economic growth, which is unproblematically taken to be the key indicator of 'social progress', can be attained (Levett et al., 2003). Advertising and the marketing of mass-manufactured goods reproduce the system by driving increased consumption, and do so by masking the true social relations of production, generating false needs that reverberate around materialistic values but fail to increase subjective senses of well-being. Ironically, part of the 'consumer attitude' is that the solution to personal fulfilment is thought to be found in the consumption of more, not less (Bauman, 1988).

Other accounts highlight how particular social and economic changes have led to significant shifts in the priorities and objectives of social actors in daily life, and how our identities are formed and maintained. Instead of identity and social status being anchored through one's role in a moral community or in relation to the means of production (such as occupational status), it is now more readily formed in relation to consumption (Veblen, 1998 [1899]); Bourdieu, 1984). In such circumstances it is not surprising that volumes of consumption have increased.

A third set of explanations focuses more specifically on the contemporary ordering of ways of life, describing a society where individuals have little option but to consume in unsustainable ways if they are to participate fully in that society (Levett et al., 2003). Cars are necessary to reach work, to obtain food, to deliver children to school; owning a variety of clothes is required in order to enter diverse social contexts without 'sticking out'; there is no alternative to having a highly mechanized kitchen. All are consequences of the socio-technical and normative ordering of daily life.[1]

Proposed policy responses to the problem of sustainability typically fall into four, not mutually exclusive, categories. One is to provide relevant product information, on the assumption that rational and informed consumers will purchase more environmentally friendly products. The second is based on the assumption that much consumption is embedded within cultural understandings that hold individualistic and materialistic values in higher esteem than collective and ecological ones. The solution is ethical conversion, persuading people away from consumerist towards ecological concerns. A third is regulation of markets in order to provide signals and incentives for consumers (for example, 'green taxation'). The fourth is to rely on technological fixes, and the innovation of less resource-intensive goods, services and systems of provision as substitutes for existing products and arrangements.

Our objective in this chapter is not to argue that such policy recommendations are worthless – each has its place within the sustainability agenda. But we are sceptical of their effectiveness because of their underlying assumptions about consumption. There is a dominant conceptualization of the consumer which underpins strategies for sustainable consumption. It postulates autonomous individuals continually exercising choice and making decisions on the basis of their personal perceptions of needs and wants, subject almost solely to constraints of time and money. We question this framework, arguing that most consumption is collectively and normatively derived, and conducted routinely in the context of socially differentiated conventions of practice. Strategies for changing patterns of consumption depend ultimately on the transformation of practices.

We take showering, whose consequences for resource allocation are formidable, as an example of ordinary consumption.[2] We argue that exploration of the habit of showering cannot be reduced to technical or infrastructural developments, but neither could it be anticipated on the basis of individual choices. Rather, it can be better explained in terms of the routinization of the practice and its interrelationship with broader socio-cultural changes that together reconfigure the way people go about cleaning bodies. The practice as it has developed is complex and embedded. The example implies that to reduce sustainable consumption to a matter of individual choices, conversion of lifestyles or market regulation overlooks the processes through which modes of consumption become embedded in conventions of daily practice.

THE LIMITED AUTONOMY OF THE CONSUMER

Consumption according to neo-classical economic theory is subject to a series of relatively straightforward calculations. Rational consumers will weigh up the products offered within any given market place and make a choice based on calculations of utility, price and the amount of time available in which to purchase and use the product (Friedman, 1957; Swann, 2002). In market exchange, consumer preferences determine what can be sold. Consumption is therefore the articulation of aggregate consumer demand under given material circumstances, and the consumer is constituted as a calculating and autonomous individual. Such a model has had significant implications for popular contemporary formulations of consumer choice. It is an instructive example of the pervasive ideological effects of the discipline of economics on current understandings of social life (for example Callon, 1998).

Conceptualizing consumption in terms of choice implies that individual behaviour is responsive and can be modified by restructuring the flow of information and incentives, or through education (Ekins, 2003). For example the European Commission's (1992) Fifth Environmental Action Programme (FEAP) states: 'policies should be developed in a way which will help consumers to make informed choices on the basis of safety, quality, durability, and general environmental implications'. It is not in question that individuals exercise choice, but a matter of how to guide and influence those choices. Again: 'Consumers can have a huge impact on sustainable development through their influence as purchasers. But they need help to make choices' (DETR, 1998a, p. 28). Such a view fails to consider how consumption is embedded in the way that different social groups engage in practices and that practices are almost always shared enterprises that are performed in the (co-)presence of others and therefore subject to collective norms of contextualized engagement.

Brown and Cameron (2000) do recognize the shared basis of the process of consuming, but nevertheless still take the model of consumers as individual decision-makers. They suggest that strategies for sharing offer a way of encouraging and informing consumers to take advantage of joint consumption schemes (like car-sharing pools). They argue that extending such schemes requires more effective communication strategies, promoting the personal gains that one feels from reciprocity and the opportunities to interact with similar-minded people. For Brown and Cameron (2000, p. 31), such communication strategies have the added benefit 'of assuring group members that others are willing to cooperate, as individuals who want to cooperate often fail to do so because they fear others will act self-interestedly and take advantage of them'. This is a story of recognizing the limits of 'commercial marketing' communication strategies and focusing on an appeal to rational individuals to enter communal modes of provision. It is still however autonomous individuals who need to be persuaded of the personal gains to be obtained from cooperation.

From this point of view, it matters what kinds of social values people hold. Many critics identify values as a principal obstacle to the achievement of sustainable consumption. Goodwin et al. (1997) observe that a 'consumeristic society' is one which holds material goods to be the primary means of achieving happiness. Elkins (1991) argues that 'overconsumption' results from the mistaken belief that 'the possession and use of an increasing number and variety of goods and services is the principal cultural aspiration and the surest route to personal happiness, social status, and national success'. And Reisch (2001, p. 369) suggests that 'changes in deeply rooted values and lifestyles' will only occur when and if 'people become enlightened consumers who learn to identify those goods whose consumption adds little or nothing to welfare'. But the problem is the obstinate persistence of values.

Such considerations lead Sanne (2002) to suggest a second solution, that environmental sustainability requires society to 'unmake' consumer culture. Among the interrelated strategies for doing so are consumer initiatives, advertising regulation, provision of collective services and a reinstitutionalization of work time. This differs from a simple reliance on informed consumer choice because it highlights the need for structural change and regulation rather than relying on autonomous and rational action at the level of the individual. It correctly acknowledges that decisions are constrained by the organization of social institutions (such as work), infrastructures (particularly transport) and commercial marketing. However, all strategies still work from within the conceptualization of individual consumers making decisions; changing the constraints is no more than a means to provide opportunities for autonomous choice based on non-consumeristic values (Stern et al., 1995; Sanne, 2002).

A third variant, ecological modernization theory, brings together consumer choice and the notion of 'elective lifestyles'. Social change during the 1960s and its reflection in the tradition of cultural studies resulted in the hugely influential proposal that consumption is no longer simply about use and function but is expressive and symbolic. The model of a 'heroic consumer' postulated that individuals have greater opportunity to decide who they want to be, projecting their identity by adopting personal styles of consumption:

> Self-identity ... is not something that is just given ... but something that has to be routinely created and sustained in the reflexive activities of the individual ... It is *the self as reflexively understood by the person in terms of her or his biography*. (Giddens, 1991a, pp. 52–3)

The proliferation and increased variety of goods available within global markets mean that those with similar economic resources are presented with a range of lifestyles from which to choose. Consumption becomes not simply a choice about goods and services but a choice about a style of life, about who we are and how we wish to be perceived by others in particular social settings (Giddens, 1991a; Featherstone, 1991a). According to Bauman (1988) there is enormous flexibility in selecting for oneself a lifestyle; one elects who to be and where to belong.

If this were the case, election to a green lifestyle would be appealing. If ecological concerns were diffused among a significant proportion of society, and providing the socio-political and infrastructural context was in place so that people had real opportunities to make green lifestyle choices, consumers as reflexive citizens would provide the basis for 'bottom-up' greening. Appropriate behaviour might include forms of grass-roots involvement in both the production and consumption of ecologically sensitive lifestyles, such as consumers who opt for green electricity tariffs and in some cases may at times turn provider by selling green power back to the grid using photovoltaic systems (Van Vliet, 2002). This would also imply people actively and reflexively monitoring the environmental profiles of different sectors of their life (Spaargaren, 1997). Georg's (1999) study of eco-villagers demonstrates that members quickly become attuned to the norms and rules of appropriate environmental behaviour. What begin as reflexively formed eco-criteria for lifestyles might then diffuse into practical consciousness and become a normative aspect of daily social life (Spaargaren, 1997).

Whether the implications for sustainability are centred around informing and guiding consumer choice, converting consumerist values or supporting reflexive eco-consumers, what remains undisputed in these approaches is that consumption is, in some way or another, an exercise of individual choice, whether by shopping or in the forging of lifestyles. Some accounts, like ecological modernization, present sophisticated recognition of the shared and routine sides of consumption: that consumers are also producers and their preferences are historically and culturally shaped. Others recognize discursive, ideological and institutional constraints, but still view consumption as the outcome of elective lifestyle choices – and what therefore need to change are the values upon which such choices rest. Explanations of consumption behaviour remain dependent upon models of individual cognitive decision-making about what or how to consume. In our view this underestimates the normative basis of shared ways of consuming, how those patterns are established in the first place, the range of purposes for which goods and services are utilized, and their role in the practices in which they are deployed.

THE COLLECTIVE, NORMATIVE AND ROUTINE ELEMENTS OF CONSUMPTION

Whether consumption preferences represent autonomous lifestyle choices or are determined by social position is a question that litters sociological debate. It is rather surprising that the sustainability agenda has drawn largely from the conceptualizations of consumption presented by the former side of this debate. Levett et al. (2003) provide an indication as to why this might be the case. They explain how neo-classical economic interpretations of choice, growth, freedom, consumption and quality of life go hand in hand, as reflected by the interchangeable ways in which these terms are used in public debate. Faced with such rhetoric, those concerned with 'green consumption' face the task of tackling such ideas head on (hence accounts of consumerism as false needs), or working within the model to advocate more or less radical measures (for example market regulation or informing choice), or focusing on resource productivity and efficiency (technical fixes and substitution within existing systems of provision), with the objective of changing infrastructural constraints and opening more avenues for the pursuit of green lifestyles.

Theories which emphasize the structural organization of consumption suggest modes of explanation currently under represented in the sustainability agenda. We address three. The first focuses on social constraints and the normative regulation of consumption. The second emphasizes the routine aspects of many ordinary or mundane forms of consumption. The third identifies and analyses integrative social practices. Together these approaches provide alternative approaches to the process of consumption which dispense with the model of the consumer as an autonomous agent making individual choices, whether in accordance with an elective lifestyle or not.

Constraints

Three types of social constraints affect consumer behaviour. The first concerns resources: economic, cultural and social resources are deployed in the process of consumption, and impact on what and how people consume. Second are normative constraints which focus on the requirements of 'fitting in' and the importance of contextual competence. The third type relates to the material and infrastructural arrangements, such as the spatial proximity of services, which condition 'choice sets'.

The work of Pierre Bourdieu (1984, 1997) offers a useful way of appreciating the effects of resources. For Bourdieu, resources (which he calls capitals) predispose different social groups to consume in ways particular to their social class position. Economic capital refers to an individual's wealth – an obvious constraint on choices of consumption. Cultural capital refers to knowledge of, engagement in and judgement about 'consecrated' cultural practices, a simple example being the preference of those with higher capital for the fine arts. Social capital refers to social connections; the types of network that any individual has available to them influences how they consume. Together, economic, cultural and social capital constrain the choices available to individuals. Money, cultural orientations and networks influence access to, judgement of and the satisfactions received by engaging in different forms of consumption.

Norms of social interaction represent a second set of constraints on consumption. These include contextual competence, and understanding and appropriating the rules of engagement in any practice. The challenges faced by the socially mobile when attempting to fit into unfamiliar contexts (Lamont, 1992), and the difficulties of being accepted within a community (Elias and Scotson, 1956; Wight, 1993) illustrate that how people consume is shaped by their capacity to read and comply with the norms and expected competencies of any given context. Normative constraints operate not only in face-to-face interaction. In their research of consuming for the home, Madigan and Munro (1996) highlight how:

> Questions of style, design and tastefulness evidently cause anxiety, but they are largely subsumed by familial values (a relaxed, comfortable haven) and also by the desire to maintain 'respectability through maintaining high house-keeping standards'. (p. 47)

Social norms are particularly powerful mechanisms of constraint when it comes to choices of consumption. They constrain in relation to social contexts, the particularities of group-based interactions, and in terms of broader culturally embedded conventions that are captured by terms such as 'respectability', 'pride' and 'reputation'.

Infrastructures and the material organization of spaces represent a third set of constraints on consumption. At a very basic level, the availability of gas and/or electricity will affect how people heat their homes, while the kinds of services available within a town will determine the range of consumption options available to its residents. More significant is how material arrangements and infrastructures condition what Levett et al. (2003) call 'choice sets':

> the 'package deal' of choices which are available as a result of a particular set of policies, and which preclude other choices. A choice set is a collection of interconnected acts of consumption, and other behaviours that come with them, and the production and infrastructure that supports them *[sic]*. (p. 42)

Choice sets can be related to 'path-dependency', where certain paths of development or action close off others. The important point is that particular infrastructural and material arrangements close off alternative forms of action. Changing modes of food provisioning provide an example. The emergence of supermarkets has brought many benefits to the individual consumer – greater variety of products at relatively cheaper prices (Harvey, 2002). However, with this apparent increase in choice has come the moving out of food retailers from local communities, reducing options of where to shop, how frequently and so on. To say that people have individual choice when food shopping is to work with a particularly limited interpretation of the word 'choice', and to ignore the socio-technical infrastructures that underlie and condition those choices in the first place.

Routines

Much consumption is routine and not subject to the forms of decision-making and reflection associated with the autonomous consumer. Lupton for example (1996, p. 155) demonstrates how 'food preferences may be acted upon in a totally unthinking way, as the product of acculturation and part of the habits of everyday life'. Ilmonen (2001) explains why routine forms of consumption do not require constant reflection. He uses the examples of grammar and recipes as instances of sets of formal rules that guide action. It is only after exhaustive rule-following conduct, like the use of language or continuous following of the same recipe, that the practice becomes habitualized and the need to reflect on recipe or grammar (which represents an encumbrance to practical action) disappears. Once this happens, the premise that action follows reflective thought is overturned; it is through the doing of the action that the rules associated with the practice are reproduced, rather than the conscious following of the rule.

That much consumption is routine and not subject to decision-making problematizes the hope that informing consumer choice will achieve sustainable consumption. Of course routines can and do change. Theories of elective lifestyles imply that change results from the reflexive application of styles of consumption. For example, ecological modernization emphasizes how eco-friendly lifestyles are critical because they provide a means through which daily routines can change. But this is plausible only if individuals can readily shift from one lifestyle to another. As the previous section argues, any radical change to lifestyles requires similar changes to an individual's volumes of resources, and to the infrastructural and material arrangements that constrain consumption. Of equal significance are the social consequences of appropriating a new lifestyle. To change a lifestyle an individual must quickly learn and appropriate new rules of behaviour and norms of conduct in order to fit in with their new lifestyle group. Even if it is possible to rapidly appropriate nuanced and context-specific rules and norms, this still leaves the actor open to social sanctions with respect to their 'established' social networks with whom they no longer share lifestyle orientations.

Even if one rejects the constraints-based explanation of consumption, theories of elective lifestyles offer little succour for the sustainability agenda. On the one hand, if there were few social consequences to changing one's lifestyle or identity, then there would be little to stop individuals from abandoning an eco-friendly lifestyle to something potentially less sustainable. On the other hand, if it is accepted that social constraints and consequences do restrict the capacity to readily change lifestyle, then the major theoretical premise (that individuals can readily shift between lifestyles) of accounts of elective lifestyles collapses.

Integrative Practices

Consumption takes place in the pursuit of practices; we consume goods and services in order to take part in or accomplish a huge variety of activities. As argued above, many practices are routine and contain their own constraints: we can only drive cars, in the large part, along designated roads, and we are required to obey the rules and regulations of that practice. Playing sport, conducting domestic chores, working in an office, are all practices that come with their own constraints and logic.

Participation in any practice requires particular forms of consumption, not as a choice but as a necessity of the practice. Equipment is necessary for most sports. Gifts are culturally regarded as essential for purposes of reciprocity when invited to friends' homes for dinner. All consumption is integrated within sets of social practices. There is no choice about whether to consume, the choice is whether to participate in the practice. Of course the products required in the pursuit of a practice can be substituted with less damaging ones. Yet substitution is only really a possibility for sustainability when the volume of that consumption is static. To substitute leaded with unleaded petrol is a positive policy, but when the volume of cars on the road and the length of journeys simultaneously increase there is no overall benefit. In such cases, focusing on the choices that people make when going about singular acts of consumption, buying petrol, is to miss the broader and more important point that it is not in acts of consumption that environmental problems are located, but in the engagement in social practices that are interconnected in terms of the types of consumption involved, and the cultural meanings and significance of the practice.

Practices are also interconnected. Any given practice shapes related practices. Ways of cooking shape both the consumption of kitchen equipment, evaluations of the types of restaurants one might desire to visit, the places that people might shop for foods and so on. Likewise preferences for ways of eating are likely to impact on how people cook, the location of eating at home (the dining table, kitchen table, lounge and so on) and the rituals that surround mealtimes. Such integration of practices suggests that it is impossible to isolate choices of consumption. Rather, the meaning, significance and ways of engaging in such practices represent a complex arrangement of cultural understandings about the interconnection of those practices which, in one way or another, rule out other ways. Thinking in terms of the logic and consumption-related dependencies of integrated practices makes the issue of consumer choice and elective lifestyles even more problematic; consumption cannot be assumed to be autonomous in the face of culturally embedded requirements and interconnected social practices that make social participation in daily life possible and meaningful.

Summary

Conceptualizing consumption as socially constrained, normatively governed, susceptible to routinization and the outcome of integrative practices, questions the value of using a model of the consumer built upon autonomous and individual choices. The implications for the sustainability agenda are profound, suggesting that the task of shifting patterns of consumption towards an eco-friendly norm is far more complex than notions of information provision, lifestyle conversion, market regulation or technological fixing (taken on their own) imply. The complex history of showering in the UK exemplifies the routinization of an ordinary form of consumption, showing how unsustainable consumption practices become embedded in the infrastructural and socio-technical arrangements of daily life.

THE RISE OF SHOWERING: INFRASTRUCTURE, TECHNOLOGY AND PRACTICE

Let us first justify the claim that showering constitutes a significant problem for engendering sustainable consumption. Briefly, there is evidence that people in the UK are showering more than ever before and that they are using more powerful showers. In 1997 showering accounted for just 36 per cent of the water used for personal hygiene (Shouler et al., 1997). But forecasts of future trends anticipate a fivefold increase in the number of litres used for showering between 1991 and 2021, accompanied by an equally dramatic decline in the use of the bath (Herrington, 1996, p. 35). Power showers pump out between 20 and 50 litres a minute, and with an average showering time of seven to eight minutes the water and energy consumption associated with daily routines of this kind soon exceeds that of a twice- or thrice-weekly bath, each bath consuming an average of 80 litres of water however long the bather spends (Turton, 1998). Such developments are clearly significant for domestic energy and water consumption.

To show that showering is best considered not simply a matter of individual choice but as embedded within complex infrastructural, technological and social arrangements, we sketch three ways of accounting for showering's erratic history: technological innovation, shifting cultural understandings of bodies and the changing social organization of temporality. Importantly, none of these accounts can be taken to be singularly causal or a primary driver. Rather, the ascendancy of showering involves a contingent coalescence of specific material, conventional and temporal elements, which are in turn mediated and reformulated through practice (see Hand et al., 2003).

Three Accounts of the Emergence of Showering

Technological innovation

To simplify, there were three key developments: the emergence of domestic plumbing, the electrification of the home and the development of power showers. The first infrastructures of showering were part of an architecture of public bathing in which the 'shower-bath', consisting of a cascade of water falling from an overhead outlet, was distinguished from general bathing in communal pools during the Greco-Roman period (Webb and Suggitt, 2000). In the eighteenth and nineteenth centuries, the expansion of urban areas and associated initiatives in sanitary science and engineering brought piped water to public conduits (Webb and Suggitt, 2000; Wright, 1960; Melosi, 2000). Despite this, it was not until the 1930s that middle-class homes were routinely equipped with hot and cold running water, and not until the 1950s for the working classes (Hardyment, 1988; Webb and Suggitt, 2000; Wright, 1960).

The electrification of UK homes was another key development and from the 1940s through to the 1960s, the Electrical Development Association (EDA)[3] explicitly promoted the immediacy of electrically powered devices (boilers, immersion heaters and, later, showers). Together, household plumbing and electricity are important elements in the material configuration of showering as we recognize it today (Schwartz-Cowan, 1983).

While such infrastructural developments are undoubtedly significant, they do not in themselves explain changes in shower technology, the increasing popularity of showering or the emergence of the power shower. There were few notable developments in shower technology until electric wall-mounted shower units became available in the 1970s. These were relatively easy to install and were initially viewed as an optional extra – something that might be added over the bath tub without changing either the purpose or the basic architecture of the bathroom. Having acquired a foothold in this manner, the shower has since become a more dominant force within the bathroom. During the 1980s and 1990s, dedicated shower cubicles and en suite arrangements became increasingly popular. Within these 'hyper-privatized' spaces, the power shower, incorporating a pump to increase the force of the water on the body, has come into its own (Shove, 2003; Webb and Suggitt, 2000).

This account of the infrastructural reorganization of showering from the communal arrangements of antiquity to its hyper-private form of today suggests that showering has been moulded by a series of interdependent technological innovations. But an exclusively materialist narrative has obvious limitations. For example, how is it that although key elements of the infrastructure were in place in the 1950s, sometimes earlier, showers did not became popular until the 1970s? More challenging still, how might we understand the use, meaning and significance – not just the availability – of showering technology?

Bodies and selves

The second account explains the changing significance of showering with reference to a cultural history of the body. The guiding assumption here is that different forms of washing are deemed appropriate depending upon how the body is experienced and understood: as something requiring 'regeneration' and 'care' in antiquity (Foucault, 1984; Sennett, 1994), as a locus of disease requiring protection, monitoring and intervention in modernity (Foucault, 1997; Vigarello, 1988), or as a site for multiple, possibly reflexive, modes of self-representation including 'fitness' and 'make-over' in contemporary culture (Bauman, 2000; Featherstone, 1991b, 1995; Giddens, 1991b).

Cultural regimes of the kind listed do not constitute homogeneous or ready-made bundles of belief and action that people simply absorb. Many actors have a stake in contesting and defining what kinds of bodies should be 'produced'. For example a feature of the nineteenth and twentieth centuries was the body (and its associated self) as a primary object of 'government' (Dean, 1999; Foucault, 1997; Rose, 1989). Bodies, as constituting the population at large, were taken to be legitimate objects of state intervention, such as public health acts and programmes of instruction and advice. Cleanliness thus became an emergent discourse important in distinguishing social classes, 'civilizing' the population and building national identities

(Bushman and Bushman, 1988; Forty, 1986; Lupton and Miller, 1992; McClintock, 1994; Shove, 2003).

Others like Beck et al. (1994) suggest that the social significance of self-disciplined bodily hygiene has not disappeared but has been reformulated in terms of the escalating risks of late-modernity. Accordingly, bodies are perceived to be at risk from rogue elements (chemicals, toxins, additives and so on) and require continual self-monitoring and maintenance. Though now framed in terms of an increasingly personalized model of responsible agency, the idea of the body as a site of social and moral reform remains important. Contemporary discourses of the body suggest that it also requires a mixture of relaxation and invigoration as well as protection from the circulating risks of techno-science and environmental degradation. Showering occupies a distinctive niche within this discursive regime, being distinguished from bathing in terms of the precise action of water on the body and an associated rhetoric of invigoration, freshness and fitness.

This second account of the ascendance of showering presupposes that dominant discourses of the body are internalized and reproduced in the way that people shower and in the meaning and significance accorded to that practice. Showering seems to offer qualities and experiences that have come to be particularly valued in contemporary culture. To understand why this might be the case, we need to turn to issues of temporality and domestic organization.

Immediacy and convenience
A key difference between bathing and showering is that the latter is now associated with speed, immediacy and convenience. There is nothing about the shower itself that makes it necessarily quick. The fact that showering is now valued for its speed and convenience is, however, in keeping with a general societal concern about what has been termed a 'time squeeze' (DEMOS, 1995; Cross, 1993; Schor, 1992; Hewitt, 1993; Linder, 1970). While there is considerable debate as to whether people have less free time now than at points in the past, there is a popular consensus that everyday life feels increasingly 'harried' (Southerton and Tomlinson, 2003).

An important characteristic of this sense of 'time squeeze' is the notion that time is a precious commodity that can be organized and managed through the careful sequencing of daily life (Southerton, 2003). As Schwartz-Cowan (1983) describes, labour-saving devices are addressed to this cultural preoccupation and also contribute to its perpetuation. While some devices have made it possible to reduce the amount of time devoted to specific tasks, the frequency with which those tasks are undertaken has often increased. The net result is that temporal schedules are crammed with small moments and episodes of attention. In this cultural context the ability to take a five-minute shower acquires its particular appeal. Showering can be slotted into narrow time frames, like those between waking in the morning and leaving for work: time slots from which bathing is deemed excluded. As such the shower belongs to a set of domestic devices whose popularity has grown precisely because they promise to help people cope with the temporal challenges of late-modern life (Warde, 1999).

Conceptualizing the increasing popularity of showering in these terms shows that practices are not determined by technological innovation or bodily considerations alone. While showering can in principle be a rapid or a lengthy affair, it is only in relation to concerns about a time squeeze that its qualities as a technology of convenience have been understood as such.

Showering as Practice

Each of these three separate, if parallel, accounts emphasizes what we might think of as a different aspect or dimension of showering. Yet all these elements are necessary conditions for the possibility of showering practice as we know it. In other words, specific arrangements of social, cultural and material entities described in the three accounts make possible the specific forms of understanding, 'know-how' and purpose that constitute showering.

To justify this claim we need to backtrack a little. The key moments in the accounts are: the reframing of cleanliness in moral discourses of the late nineteenth century; the wide-spread provisioning of piped water and electricity infrastructures that reached the majority of the population in the 1950s; the rearticulation of bodies as sites of self-monitoring and maintenance; and the emergent discourses of harriedness in the 1980s. Most simply, this piecing together of key moments illustrates how infrastructures are only one relatively small, albeit crucial, part of the puzzle that explains the emergence of a resource-intensive practice. It also suggests that to conceptualize these changes in terms of individual consumer choice, or the presence of flawed consumerist values or even emerging ecological reflexivity, would be one-sided. In the last case for instance, the potential for ecologically framed self-transformation when juxtaposed against powerful convictions regarding personal health, moral well-being and social respectability seems limited.

While a full critical deconstruction of the linearity of this story (the 'reverse engineering' of the rise of showering) is beyond the scope of this chapter, we can at least observe that the practice of showering has co-evolved with infrastructural and technological developments, changing moral regimes of cleanliness and the body, in the context of temporal organization and experiences of daily life. Showers did not seem so attractive when the technology and infrastructures first became available. To suggest that the time lag was due to some diffusion curve effect and that for utilitarian reasons showering must necessarily have become popular is to ignore the cultural and social specificities of the practice. Rather, the story is one of how changing techniques, know-how and ways of understanding bodily cleanliness created a space for showering to challenge the previously dominant way of doing bodily cleansing (that is bathing). From this vantage point we can see how the practice has unfolded, become differentiated from bathing, and sedimented as one alternative among interconnected and partly equivalent practices. Showering came to be understood as a means to invigorate and a conduit to speed and convenience. As such, showering has emerged not simply as a substitute for bathing but as a practice with its own logics and requirements – power showers highlight its invigorating properties over relaxation, shower cubicles exemplify its symbolic status as a 'private practice', and standing up rather than lying down symbolizes its brevity.

Approaching the rise of showering from a practice-centred perspective illuminates how infrastructures, and ordinary consumption more generally, raise a very different set of questions than does a focus on more conspicuous forms of consumption. Infrastructures and the habits of ordinary consumption are embedded in cultural conventions of a type where continual reflexive lifestyle monitoring or expansive consideration of the range of options when going about consumption is not practicably possible. Indeed the case of showering suggests that, except for heuristic purposes, it would be misguided to separate lifestyles, modes of provision (for example public/state or private/domestic), cultural ideas (for example about comfort, cleanliness and convenience – see Shove, 2003) and social values. The performative dynamics of each are inextricably related. Thus we suggest a focus on how practices change offers a better route towards understanding how conventions and routines become established in daily life in ways that become taken for granted, unavoidable and necessary.

CONCLUSION

We have suggested that 'individual choice' within final consumption is a restrictive notion for understanding the complexity of social practices involving the appropriation of goods and services. Consumption is embedded within routine and normative practices which are constituted as much through collective as through self-reflexive individual action. This is particularly the case with ordinary, inconspicuous forms of consumption. This is precisely the nature of the consumption of infrastructures, and the use of such resources is in most cases hidden because it is embedded within particular practices. This analysis therefore suggests that changing or modifying individual orientations towards more environmentally sustainable consumption is a task that stretches far beyond the provision of more options or more information regarding the environmental implications of those choices.

We have also argued that many ordinary forms of consumption are governed by norms and conventions which are constituted and reproduced through practice in the conduct of daily life. Conceiving consumption as a part of practice offers a framework for appreciating how norms and conventions of consumption become established in the routines of daily life. As demonstrated by showering, examining how a practice unfolds allows for the identification of key elements that configure the possibility and establishment of a novel set of conventions. These are the processes through which practices change, new practices emerge, separate and become interlocked with others. These are processes that condition what Levett et al. (2003) refer to as 'choice sets'. Similarly the way we understand and engage in any practice will set the conditions and range of options for how we engage and understand other practices. For example the emergence of showering and its symbolic representation as invigorating have redefined the purpose of the bath as something for relaxation, often positioning the former as a daily and the latter as a more infrequent practice.

From the viewpoint of final consumption, consideration of more sustainable forms of consumption of services requires an understanding of the complex and embedded nature of social practices. There are no doubt some individuals who are self-starters in light of ethical principles related to the environment. However, such individuals represent only a small proportion of people in the face of a huge collective issue. Even if a greater range of environmentally sustainable products are made available, revision of the normalized social practices that consume such resources is not high on the list of priorities. In short, neither wider choices nor information aimed at changing individual lifestyles are likely to be sufficient to disrupt the embedded nature of consumption patterns within the daily lives of most people. Making consumption sustainable is a different, and more intractable, problem than it appears in the terms of orthodox accounts of the sovereign consumer.

NOTES

1. For a more comprehensive discussion of explanations for the emergence of an unsustainable consumer culture see Shove and Warde (2002).
2. See Gronow and Warde (2001) for a detailed discussion of 'ordinary consumption'.

3. The Electrical Development Association was founded under the Electricity Act of 1919, and
   funded by the supply undertakings. From 1926 onwards, the development of domestic
   demand was a key concern of the EDA. See Forty (1986).

4. The new 'energy divide': politics, social equity and sustainable consumption in reformed infrastructures

Jane Summerton[1]

It is Monday morning and I am about to start writing a chapter for a new anthology on sustainable consumption in technical infrastructures. As I reach idly for my coffee cup and saunter towards my desk, I take a glance at the morning newspaper that lies half-opened on the kitchen table. An article on the first page catches my eye. It shows a determined-looking woman sitting at her kitchen table in another part of town. This winter is bitterly cold, and the woman's rented apartment is scantily insulated against the freezing winds. The costs of heat, lighting and hot water are skyrocketing, and she is having trouble paying her power bills. The newspaper article speculates that we will soon witness an 'energy divide' – that is, a new type of schism between the haves and have-nots of infrastructural services. While the former have access to an abundant supply of energy on reasonable terms, the latter lack basic access to such energy on terms that are affordable to them. The woman in the newspaper is resourceful however, and determined to keep her energy costs down. The newspaper reports on the various steps she has taken to reduce her consumption: turned down her thermostat to 19 degrees, closed off a room that she doesn't use every day, and put in new sealing tape along all her windows. She is taking active steps to avert another high electricity bill.

INTRODUCTION

This chapter focuses on changing forms of infrastructural provision in the energy sector and their implications for a particular group of consumers, namely low-income or 'economically vulnerable' consumers. Drawing on developments in Scandinavia, the UK and parts of the USA, the chapter critically discusses managerial practices and consumer responses that have emerged from recent reform policies in electricity. What are the implications of the changing utility practices for different groups of consumers? Which consumers are successfully availing themselves of new service options and which consumers are marginalized or neglected? To what extent can tendencies towards a polarizing of infrastructural consumption, an 'energy divide', be discerned in various places? What are the links between sustainable consumption and social equity in technical infrastructures?

The chapter is organized as follows. First I will discuss some recent changes in infrastructural practices that have strong relevance for low-income consumers, drawing on emergent experiences from policy reforms in the UK, Scandinavia and parts of the USA. Then I will take a closer look at specific patterns, managerial practices and consumer responses in the context of Sweden's electricity reform, which illustrates many of the core issues of the chapter. In conclusion the chapter explores implications for our understandings of politics, policy and sustainable consumption in technical infrastructures.

POLICY REFORMS IN TECHNICAL INFRASTRUCTURES

Starting in the late 1980s, policy reforms aimed at reconfiguring technical infrastructures – such as electricity, postal services, air traffic, railways, taxis and telecommunications – were introduced in many Western countries. The UK (1990) and Norway (1991) were among the first to design and implement policy reforms in electricity, followed by Sweden (1996) and several other countries in Northern Europe. The UK and Sweden later (1998–99) introduced additional measures to stimulate 'full competition' by which all domestic consumers were given opportunities to choose among utility suppliers. In the United States shortly thereafter, a dramatic power shortage in California (2000–2001) became a highly publicized illustration of how policy efforts to reconfigure power systems could have strong economic consequences for many groups of consumers. Although these reforms and events differed in important ways, a common feature has been a rhetorical political emphasis on increasing the opportunities for consumer choice to the presumed benefit of all consumers. Often related to these opportunities, a shared expectation of many infrastructural reforms is that consumers will pay less for their power than before.

When approaching the issue of how infrastructural reforms can be understood from a consumer perspective, it is important to keep at least two things in mind. First, it is clear that the shaping of specific policy processes – their politics, designs and practices – differs in specific local and national contexts and can have many different kinds of implications for consumers. Also, in the interweaving of policy processes with many other situational factors, it is not always clear which developments are related to specific policy changes and which are not. For example while in some cases radical changes in consumer prices for electricity can be linked to specific deregulation policies, in other cases this linkage is not causal or straightforward. Any discussion of consumer impacts of infrastructural reforms must therefore pay careful attention to differences in contextual dynamics and patterns. Second, as this chapter will show, it is important to distinguish between different groups of consumers and the ways in which aspects of their life situations contribute to their (differential) opportunities as consumers. For example the UK's National Consumer Council has identified a number of situational factors that contribute to what is referred to as 'fuel poverty' among consumers – including high energy prices relative to income, low energy efficiency of the home and family circumstances (such as being a single parent, having a disability or lacking capital) (National Consumer Council, 1993, p. 73). Such factors starkly illustrate the heterogeneity of consumers and their life situations, as well as how different mechanisms may serve to reinforce social inequities.

Three phenomena illustrate some of the implications of new infrastructural politics for low-income consumers. These are: (1) changing managerial practices that exclude low-income or 'less lucrative' consumers; (2) increases in energy prices that impact strongly upon low-income consumers because these consumers pay proportionately more for their energy; and (3) indications that low-income consumers are underrepresented among 'active' consumers in re-regulated electricity infrastructures.

Changing Managerial Practices: Mechanisms of Exclusion?

Historically, managerial practices in infrastructures have been guided by the ethos of universal service provision – that is, the notion that all consumers are entitled to the same goods and services on essentially equal terms. The traditional view of utilities and their regulators as providers 'of and for the public good' has been a deeply embedded cultural value in most sectors. This ethos has been increasingly challenged however by recent policy reforms that have signalled new roles for utilities and utility managers. As Chappells et al. (2000) observe:

> The key shift instigated by the privatisation and liberalisation of utility markets has been the replacement of the ethic of public service – the ideal of

cheap, reliable, universal access to utility services for all irrespective of
income or location – with the goal of *profitability*. (p. 17, emphasis added)

This transition is having strong implications for utility–consumer relations.
Utility managers are increasingly differentiating their goods and services
among different groups of consumers, based on these consumers' perceived
economic value to the utility. The targeting of attractive users often entails
'lifestyle marketing' of specific socio-economic groups and networked
spaces (Guy et al., 1997). The resulting splintering of infrastructural
networks in spatial, institutional and social terms is expressed in both the
niche marketing of goods and services to lucrative local consumers, and
increased social polarization. Specifically with regard to energy, Graham and
Marvin (1994) have shown in a study of managerial strategies in parts of
Great Britain in the early 1990s how competing energy companies
systematically identified and targeted lucrative groups of consumers, who
were then offered extensive goods and services. The practice of 'cherry
picking' of attractive consumers was accompanied by the 'social dumping' of
less lucrative, poorer customers who were offered minimal goods and
services. Similar managerial practices have also been observed in Sweden,
which introduced policy measures to increase competitiveness within its
electricity system in the mid-1990s (Summerton, 2002). Utility managers
actively constructed heterogeneous identities for different groups of
consumers, based on these customers' perceived needs and interest in
specific infrastructural goods and services. While consumers with high
volumes of consumption were targeted with a diverse range of attractive
service options, consumers who had lower consumption levels were offered
only basic goods and services. In this way certain groups of consumers were
privileged while others were marginalized or neglected altogether. These
practices illustrate one of the most striking paradoxes of the Swedish policy
reform: while the rhetorical goal of the reform was to enable consumers to
choose their utilities, the result appears to be that utilities are increasingly
choosing their consumers.

The High Cost of Power: Implications for Low-Income Consumers

The second phenomenon of changing infrastructural politics that has strong
implications for low-income consumers is increases in electricity prices. Like
the choice inversion just mentioned, another paradox of some electricity
reforms concerns the high cost of power: although the political goal of
'deregulation' is often to stimulate lower prices for consumers, the result in
some areas has been a marked increase in consumer prices. For example, in
the UK's initial phase of energy policy reform (between 1990 and 1993),
consumer prices for electricity rose dramatically, impacting strongly on

household expenditures among low-income groups, who spend proportionately more on their total expenditures on energy than other consumers. In 1993, the National Consumer Council (1993, p. 73) defined certain households as 'fuel poor'; that is, 'people whose incomes are too low for them to afford the gas and electricity they need for light, warmth and cooking, and who therefore restrict their fuel consumption to less than their needs'. In short, the relative cost burden was significantly higher for low-income consumers, such as the unemployed or retired persons, compared to more affluent consumers.[2]

The emergent impacts of the opening of the UK's gas and electricity markets to domestic consumers in 1998–99 were analysed specifically with regard to low-income consumers. In a study of nearly 400 low-income households,[3] the National Right to Fuel Campaign (1999, p. 16) concluded that nearly half of the interviewed consumers reported difficulties in heating their homes, with one-half stating that they left one or more rooms unheated during cold weather. The study also notes that 'the initial opening of the electricity market does not appear to have attracted much interest' among these consumers, suggesting that the market 'is not working effectively for low-income consumers' (1999, pp. 1, 37).

The differential effect of high energy prices on poor consumers was also starkly shown during California's widely publicized statewide energy crisis in the winter and spring of 2000–2001. Following a major policy reform, California's electricity system incurred supply shortages that led to dramatic increases in consumers' costs for electricity. Many groups of vulnerable consumers were suddenly forced to drastically cut down on their consumption of energy for lighting and heating. Besides low-income consumers, these groups also included public organizations such as schools and public health clinics. The crisis was widely reported in the daily press, which warned that a divide among the 'haves' and 'have-nots' of electrical power could be increasingly discerned.[4] In addition to skyrocketing prices, poor customers in some areas were also faced with significant cuts in utilities' aid programmes for low-income households, further reducing these households' ability to pay for power.[5] To alleviate the situation, California's state regulators implemented various measures such as providing exemptions from rate increases for low-income consumers who signed up for a state-approved discount programme.[6] Numerous cities also took steps that were specifically designed to reduce energy cost burdens among the poor.[7]

The Issue of Consumer Choice: Who are the Active Consumers?

The third phenomenon that illustrates the ways in which changes in infrastructural politics are having detrimental implications for low-income consumers concerns the new opportunities of consumer choice in reformed infrastructures. A salient feature of power reforms in Scandinavia and the UK (as well as many other countries) is that consumers have the option – at least in principle – to actively choose among competing utilities and sign a contract with the utility of their choice. This new option actualizes two questions: how many consumers are active in this sense, and who are these consumers?

These questions were explored in a study of responses to the 1991 electricity reform in Norway, which was the first Scandinavian country to re-regulate its power system. In 1998 the Nordic Council of Ministers released a report of consumer responses, and the results were not encouraging from the perspective of social equity. At the time only about 7 per cent of all households had utilized the opportunity to switch to a new provider. Moreover there was a clear pattern with regard to the identities of those consumers who actively participated in this process. The characteristics of 'power shopping' consumers[8] were as follows:

- Male (70 per cent of all power shoppers)
- Between 30 and 60 years of age (about 80 per cent of all power shoppers)
- Live in single-family houses (over 75 per cent) that are often larger than average
- Have a university education (over 50 per cent)
- Have a higher average income than the control population
- Have a higher average electricity consumption than the control population.

By identifying these 'active' consumers, the study also indirectly indicated those consumers who were not active in this sense – specifically women, renters and low-income households.

Similarly a 2002 study of British consumer responses to the opening of the country's gas and electricity markets to domestic consumers in 1998/99 analysed how many consumers had switched supplier and how the ensuing economic gains had been distributed. Although the consumer collective as a whole had saved a substantial amount of money as a result of fuel switching, the benefits were unequally distributed. Only about 1 per cent of the estimated savings went to prepayment meter users (who are disproportionately low-income consumers), while over 50 per cent went to direct debit customers (who are predominantly higher-income consumers). The report concluded, 'Liberalisation is benefiting the rich substantially more than the poor' (Boardman and Fawcett, 2002, p. 18).

TAKING A CLOSER LOOK: EXPERIENCES FROM SWEDEN

Each of the three phenomena discussed above in relation to low-income consumers – that is, managerial practices that exclude them, sharp increases in energy prices that disproportionately impact upon them, and their underrepresentation as 'active' consumers – can be observed in Sweden since the country implemented its electricity policy reform in 1996. Like Norway, Sweden introduced a national reform as a means to stimulate competition in electricity generation and trade (but not power distribution, which continues to operate as a natural monopoly). Both countries are also participants in a common Nordic market arena for electricity trade, Nord Pool, which currently encompasses over 300 market actors.[9] The purpose of the Swedish electricity reform was reportedly to 'increase efficiency in production and sales by creating freedom of choice for electricity users' (Swedish National Energy Administration, 2002, p. 1). By the terms of the reform, all end-use consumers were given the right to choose among competing generating utilities[10] and negotiate with these utilities as a means to reduce their costs for power, improve their contractual terms and conditions, or gain access to a particular type of power (such as green electricity).[11]

For domestic consumers, Sweden's policy reform actually consisted of two incremental reforms. By the terms of the initial reform on 1 January 1996, any consumer who wished to switch electricity supplier was first required to have a meter that could register hour-by-hour consumption. Since these meters were expensive to buy, it was relatively costly for consumers (particularly those with low electricity consumption) to switch supplier. Following an interim reform in 1997 that established a price ceiling on such meters, the hour-by-hour meter requirement was removed altogether on 1 November 1999. It is now possible for a consumer to switch supplier at any time. The situation of choice with regard to electricity supplier is however strictly optional: those consumers who do not actively choose their suppliers continue to receive power from their existing utilities on standardized terms.

Recent Managerial Practices in Sweden

One early utility response to the Swedish policy reform was that many utilities began promoting various types of 'brand name electricity' in an attempt to distinguish their goods and services from those of other utilities, while building new images for their respective utilities. Examples of electricity brand names were 'Spektra' (promoted by Sydkraft), 'Advantage Electricity' (promoted by a municipal consortium) and 'Two Holes in the Wall' (promoted by Vattenfall). Each was intensely promoted by the respective utility. Besides differentiating among different types of power, in some cases branding also meant differentiating among groups of consumers according to their perceived interest in various goods and services – as well as their different economic value to the respective utilities. In some areas managers conceptualized new identities for different groups of consumers, based on such criteria as their volume of consumption, their type of housing, and their presumed willingness and ability to pay. While some groups were given privileged access to a range of goods and services, others were offered fewer alternatives. The new managerial practices were thus expressed in explicit segmenting, ranking and choosing among different groups of customers. These practices became a means to constitute and exploit a new politics of difference and profitability among domestic consumers.

Case studies of two early campaigns to promote brand name electricity indicated however a number of unexpected phenomena. For one thing the 'new' goods and services offered to different groups of consumers were to a great extent not new at all. Instead they were typically pre-existing infrastructural services that managers wanted to make visible to users. Also, although the campaigns represented an important shift in utility practices, they did not herald a fundamental change in the way in which managers actually categorized their consumers. Several of the 'new' consumer identities were deceptively close to the utilities' traditional boxes of standardized tariff categories for different subscriber groups. Notably, while managers tried hard to splinter their utility networks, many of the consumers refused to be persuaded and enrolled. Many consumers remained unengaged or, alternatively, 'chose not to choose'. The two case studies of branding electricity in Sweden are clear examples of consumer resistance to managerial attempts to represent their identities, preferences and practices – and to reformulate utility–consumer relationships (Summerton, 2002).

Cost of Electricity in Sweden: Exploring Heterogeneities

The cost of electricity is however an important issue for Swedish consumers. While fluctuations in price are common, the issue of how to interpret and explain such fluctuations and/or sustained price increases is complex and political. In Sweden actors with different interests typically express divergent perspectives that point to such factors as 'changes in coal and oil prices', 'extreme cold weather this winter', 'low hydro flow/dry year', 'low reserves', 'shutting down that nuclear power plant', 'increases in energy taxes', 'sign of a well-functioning, competitive power market' and 'sign of a young competitive market that does not really work yet'.[12] As in other areas of technoscience, economics and politics are co-constructed and closely intertwined.

Rather than enter this politicized arena by arguing for the links between policy reforms and power prices, I will simply focus on two aspects of price that have had particular relevance for low-income consumers in Sweden in recent years, namely:

- increases in consumer prices
- indications of how these increases have differentially affected different groups of consumers.

Before approaching these issues, it is important to explore briefly how the heterogeneity of household consumers is expressed in Sweden. A common way of categorizing such consumers is by 'average' volume of use, as indicated by what type of housing they live in and whether they use electricity to heat the house:

- consumers in single-family houses with electric space heat: 20 000 kWh/year
- consumers in single-family houses without electric space heat: 5000 kWh/year
- consumers in apartments (without electric space heat): 2000 kWh/year

Although averages like these can be misleading, these statistics show that consumers whose homes are heated by electric space heat are the heaviest users of electricity in Sweden.

What about possible links between the type of housing and disposable income; that is, how does the above category of 'single-family house' correlate with income? Even though it might be tempting to assume that consumers in single-family houses are wealthier than consumers in apartments, this is not necessarily the case. Apartment dwellers in large cities such as Stockholm and Gothenburg are often more well-to-do than homeowners in rural areas, and some owners in single-family houses (such as single mothers, couples in already amortized homes and pensioners) might have relatively low incomes. At the same time it is also misleading to conclude – as is sometimes done in consumer reports – that the heavy consumers with electric space heat are most vulnerable to price increases. It can be argued that those consumers in this group who are affluent are better equipped to absorb a large price increase than economically vulnerable consumers are to handle even a modest price increase.

One result of Sweden's power reform is that consumers now pay for power according to two different pricing mechanisms. Customers who do not sign explicit contracts with their respective utility pay an ongoing price (*tillsvidarepris*) that is applied to all customers who do not negotiate alternative terms. In contrast, customers who sign explicit power contracts pay a contract price (*kontraktspris*) that has other terms and conditions, reflecting many negotiated variables such as choices between fixed or variable price, long-term or short-term pricing, spot-pricing and the like.

What are some of the recent patterns in the cost of Swedish electricity among groups of consumers who have different situations with regard to housing, disposable income and type of utility contract? In an October 2002 report, the Swedish National Energy Administration analysed the period after the electricity reform was implemented, noting the following:

- Household prices for power were essentially the same in 1996 and late 2002.[13]
- Domestic consumers who were billed according to 'ongoing prices' had 'paid an average of 15–20 per cent more for their electricity than those consumers who had been active on the electricity market' (cost comparison April 2002).
- There are indications that generating utilities uphold the notion that the average ongoing price should be higher than the contract price for consumers in single-family dwellings (and specifically without electric space heat). It should be even higher for consumers in apartments, but lower for the high consumers in single-family dwellings (those with electric space heat).
- The average price margin among utilities in 2002 for consumers in apartments was about one-third of the total cost that these consumers paid for power.

How should these statistics be interpreted? First, they are averages that are distributed across all utilities and consumers and as such do not show actual price increases for individual consumers, which may vary considerably depending upon what utilities charge for power. For example in January 2002 the prices that Swedish utilities charged their 'ongoing' customers varied enormously from 36 öre/kWh to 111 öre/kWh (that is, from about 0.04 euros/kWh to about 0.12 euros/kWh).[14] Second, the report discussed above does not show the ways in which certain factors, specifically low income, heavy electricity consumption and ongoing price, can combine to make some consumers especially vulnerable. Bladh (2003, p. 15) has identified the proportion of disposable income that specific groups of low-income consumers pay for electricity, based on available data from Swedish Statistics. One group of low-income consumers is 'single women/men without children or income from employment', for example single pensioners and students, who live in single-family houses with high consumption (electric space heat) and who pay an ongoing price. These economically vulnerable consumers paid as much as 22–23 per cent of their disposable income on electricity in 2003. Similarly, the same categories but *with* children reportedly spent 16–17 per cent of their disposable income on power.[15]

The 'ongoing' customers are also singled out in a report by the Swedish Consumer Authority to the Swedish government in December 2002, which notes:

> The passive electricity consumers have – for most of the period during which the electricity market has been competitive – paid a so called on-going price, which for most utilities has routinely been much higher than the price of e.g. (negotiated) one-year contracts. ... The Authority finds it remarkable that *those consumers who are loyal must pay extra simply because they have not actively contracted for a better price.* (2002, pp. 10–11, emphasis added)

This critique leads us to a key aspect of the Swedish reform process from a consumer perspective, namely the choice or option of switching supplier.

Switching Supplier: How Many Consumers and Which Groups?

Besides price increases, the issue of how many and which groups of consumers actively avail themselves of various choice options in Swedish electricity is perhaps one of the most monitored aspects of the country's reform process. Utilities and their interest groups regularly carry out polls or surveys and the public authorities have released at least four major consumer reports in recent years. For example, in 2000 the Swedish National Audit Office conducted telephone interviews with almost 1400 domestic consumers about their attitudes and responses to the re-regulated electricity and telecommunications markets in Sweden. Respondents were asked if they knew about the new option of switching utility, how they had received information about this option, whether they thought it was difficult or easy to compare the offerings of competing companies, whether they had switched supplier and/or negotiated new terms with their existing supplier, and what the economic and other results of these negotiations had been. The results indicated that only 10 per cent of all domestic consumers had availed themselves of the option of switching supplier, and consumers who had high incomes and consumers who lived in single-family houses were overrepresented. The report makes the following observation:

> There is a clear tendency to polarization between active and passive consumers. This is expressed among other things in whether or not consumers have sought information, whether or not they have compared prices and offers, and whether or not they have expressed complaints of any kind. In particular, it is clear that *low income consumers* have been less active in

seeking information and making comparisons among utilities. (2000, p. 48, emphasis added)

This picture of strong polarization is confirmed by subsequent reports from the Swedish Consumer Authority in 2000 and 2002. In all of the three major consumer categories (see previous section), those consumers who had relatively high annual incomes, specifically more than about 35 000 euros, had more often been active in switching utility (2002, pp. 45–7).[16] Notably however the percentage of consumers who were active in these ways had increased significantly to about 43 per cent of all consumers in 2002 (including a massive 72 per cent of consumers in single-family houses with electric space heat). The following characteristics of consumer identities are however still overrepresented among the measurably active consumers: they are male, older (age 38 and over), have high incomes, are employed full-time or self-employed and live in detached, single-family houses. In other words, similar to the findings of the Norwegian report discussed earlier, it is the economically strong consumers who are calling their utilities, negotiating with utility managers and contracting cheap power. In contrast, economically vulnerable consumers who presumably are most in need of obtaining cheaper power are not utilizing the opportunities for reducing their costs. Instead they are paying more for their power than are other, measurably active and more affluent consumers. The Swedish Consumer Authority's report from December 2002 also notes however that even many economically 'strong' consumers are still not as active as could be desired:

Although it is a positive [sign] that so many consumers in this group are active, it must also be noted that almost one-third are passive and thus perhaps pay thousands of crowns more [for their power] than they should every year. (2002, p. 34)

CONCLUSION: CONSUMER CHOICE, POLITICS AND POLICY IN INFRASTRUCTURE – AND WHY THEY MATTER

In reflecting upon the implications of these dynamics, it is important to keep in mind that the various statistics, surveys and consumer reports are only representations of consumer identities. As such they tell us very little about these consumers' lived experiences, self-defined identities and everyday social practices. Also they embody complex chains of interpretation and translation among many actors – respondents, survey researchers, writers of consumer reports and social science researchers who publish chapters like this one.[17] Expressed another way, the ecologies of consumers – that is the textures of motives, patterns of use, strategies, struggles and passions that form the everyday life-worlds of heterogeneous individuals and households – remain hidden from view. In order to approach an understanding of what differential access and exclusion in infrastructures might mean for these consumers, it is necessary to know much more about their life conditions, their experiences of everyday life, and the patterns of meaning and practice by which these experiences are constituted.

In line with this perspective, recent social science work has emphasized the necessity of situating consumers' actions in the context of the socio-material systems of provision in which they are embedded (Chappells et al., 2000; Shove and Chappells, 2001). Consumers' practices must be understood as situated actions that take place within the structural constraints, institutional rules, and other terms and conditions that characterize the systems in question. In this chapter it has been argued that such constraints include the managerial practices by which the terms and conditions for consumers' practices are constituted, negotiated and performed.

What does the material in this chapter indicate about social equity among consumers of technical infrastructures? At least three observations can be made. The first concerns the notion of the 'sovereign consumer'. The discourse of the sovereign consumer has increasingly come to the fore as an outcome of the free market ideology that has gained strength in Europe and the United States, providing among other things political support for re-regulating infrastructural systems. This discourse draws upon neoclassic economic theory that views consumers as rational economic agents who are free and unconstrained to make their own individual choices. This chapter shows however that the idea of consumer choice is inappropriate for understanding how and why groups of people consume electricity (and perhaps other infrastructural goods and services), what their real choices are, and why there are differences in responses among social groups (see also Southerton et al., this volume). Instead consumers' choices in infrastructure systems are structured, constrained or circumscribed by many factors and mechanisms that include differential access to goods and services, discriminatory practices that link consumer services to consumer income, and more or less institutionalized means for utility providers to choose and/or differentially privilege groups of customers. Despite the best-laid plans of reform ideologies, the sovereign consumer of infrastructural commodities remains essentially a myth.

A second conclusion concerns discriminatory politics in technical infrastructures and the role of policy in dealing with this problem. The discussion about managerial practices showed the ways in which politics, difference and discrimination are actively constructed and sustained in infrastructures. Recent work in science and technology studies has focused attention on the mechanisms by which infrastructural practices can marginalize and inflict suffering upon groups of people by excluding them from access to certain goods and services or categorizing them in certain ways (Bowker and Star, 1999). It can be argued that access to life-sustaining infrastructures such as energy at affordable costs should be viewed as an integral part of all consumers' and citizens' bill of rights. Many of the infrastructural systems of daily life in the Western world are publicly owned or service-oriented operations, if not formally then at least in terms of their societal roles and responsibilities. As such they should be expected to offer their commodities to all customers on essentially equal terms.

As this chapter indicates however, the long-standing social contract between utilities and policy-makers on this point is being radically changed by the new regulatory regimes behind deregulation and other infrastructural reforms. These changes call for new types of policy measures to ensure non-discriminatory practices that protect the interests of economically vulnerable, 'non-lucrative' groups of consumers and increase the long-term social sustainability of infrastructure systems. Such policy measures might include government programmes for stimulating utility projects (for example energy monitoring, energy efficiency programmes, retrofits, system conversions) in areas with low-income housing; incentive programmes whereby households with low incomes can qualify for opportunities for choosing environmental options such as 'green electricity'; programmes to improve in concrete ways the readability of utility brochures, bills and public information in ways that enhance the accessibility of such materials; and new approaches that enable consumers to take more active but simple steps to monitor and limit their own energy consumption (such as self-monitoring procedures or shorter prepaid periods). Utilities should perhaps also be required to report to the government on a regular basis regarding the concrete steps that they are taking to ensure equitable access to their goods and services for all groups of consumers.

A third conclusion from this chapter concerns the implications of current practices for the long-term potential of encouraging sustainable consumption. This perspective raises a number of difficult questions. Will emerging utility practices that privilege high-consuming, lucrative households lead to expanded goods and services (and often higher consumption) for these groups, and limited offerings for non-lucrative, poorer groups? Is there a risk that wealthy consumers who pay less for their power will be best able to afford environmental options, while poorer consumers will not, leading to ever greater imbalances between social and ecological sustainability? Will pricing mechanisms whereby heavy users pay less for their power tend to encourage them to use even more power, thus consuming even larger parts of the total 'consumption space'? In other words will the differential effects of changing infrastructural dynamics mean that low-income consumers will assume responsibility and costs for a reduced long-term sustainable consumption, while more wealthy consumers will continue to have high consumption levels that undermine the potential for such sustainability? It is clear that the potential for long-term sustainable consumption in technical infrastructures is closely linked to issues of social equity.

Why are these issues important to understand and be acted upon? From the perspective of this chapter, it can be argued that it does matter to understand the mechanisms and practices by which some groups get privileged access to infrastructures, while others are marginalized or excluded; it does matter to recognize that economically vulnerable groups pay more for life-sustaining technological goods and services; it does matter to ask why some groups of consumers are more or less exempted from pressures to limit their levels of consumption, while other groups are forced to reduce their consumption; and it does matter to understand in what ways policy reforms can contribute to a deepening of inequities, and to explore what can be done about it.

NOTES

1. The author wishes to thank colleagues in the 'Technology, Practice, Identity' research group at Linköping University, particularly Minna Salinen-Karlsson and Jonas Anshelm, for a valuable critique of an earlier version of this chapter.
2. Besides higher relative cost burdens, the National Consumer Council (1993, p. 65) also identified three types of issues that should be addressed when considering the implications of regulatory changes on domestic consumers, namely: access (how readily can consumers get connected and stay connected?), equity (how fairly are domestic consumers treated in relation to other actors such as company shareholders?) and information (how open and accountable are the systems and their regulators?).
3. The study was conducted through interviews with nearly 400 members of a nationally recruited panel of which 'over one third ... live in poverty and over a half live in, or on the margins of, poverty'.
4. See for example *San Francisco Chronicle*, 'Municipal Utilities, Customers Shielded from State's Energy Crisis', 5 January 2001, p. B1.
5. See for example *Daily Californian*, 'Cuts in Energy Aid Worry Low-Income Locals', 20 February 2001, pp. 1, 5.
6. *Los Angeles Times*, 'US May Hike Aid for Poor's Utilities', 18 June 2001, pp. A1, A13.
7. See for example *San Francisco Chronicle*, 'Oakland Looks Ready to Cut Energy Tax', 23 March 2001, pp. A1, A20; *Daily Californian*, 'Low-Income Residents May Expect Lower Energy Bills, More Allowances', 6 February 2001, pp. 1, 4.
8. This definition is of course problematic from a social science perspective. For example, a consumer may actively decide not to be 'active' – or actively decide to be loyal to his/her utility.
9. Besides Norway and Sweden, other participants are Finland, western Denmark (Jylland and Fyn) and eastern Denmark (Själland). In April 2002 a total of 305 actors were active on Nord Pool. See Swedish Consumer Authority (2002), p. 17.
10. Notably, the distribution of electricity is still carried out in the form of regulated monopolies. This means that while consumers are free to contract among competing generating companies, the transmission and distribution of the contracted power are carried

out by distributing utilities whose roles, terms and conditions are not open to consumer choice and negotiation.

11. It is important to note however that despite the intentions of the Swedish reform, a strong systemwide concentration of ownership among a relatively small number of generating utilities still persists. This concentration is illustrated by the fact that among the country's 125–30 generating utilities, the three largest companies currently deliver electricity to approximately 70 per cent of all end-users. Perhaps paradoxically, the number of generating utilities in Sweden has decreased since the electricity reform was introduced in January 1996.

12. See for example Bladh (2002), p. 75; 'Torrår gör slut på 'elrea', *Energimagasinet*, nr 1, 2003; 'El-priset – en ruggig väderfråga', *Svensk energi.nu*, nr. 16, 6 November 2002; 'Svensk Energi.nu synar de varierande elpriserna', *Svensk energi.nu*, nr. 2, 10 February 2003.

13. Swedish prices increased markedly during the first year of the country's power reform, followed by a relatively stable period of lower prices until 2001–2003, when prices again increased. On a system level, the electricity price in 1996 (excluding taxes and distribution costs) was 26.0 öre/kWh (about 0.03 euros/kWh) as compared with an average of 12.6 öre/kWh during the period 1997–2000. See Swedish Consumer Authority (2002); 'Torrår gör slut på elrea', *Energimagasinet*, nr 1, 2003; 'El-priset – en ruggig väderfråga', *Svensk energi.nu*, nr. 16, 6 November 2002.

14. 'Svensk Energi.nu synar de varierande elpriserna', *Svensk energi.nu*, nr. 2, 10 February 2003.

15. Bladh points out that these estimates are based on available statistics on electricity prices in 2003 and disposable income in 2001, which means that there is a risk of a slight inaccuracy in the results.

16. The definition of 'active' consumer that is used here (and in most surveys) focuses on whether or not the consumer has contacted her/his utility to contract for new terms and/or switched supplier.

17. In this regard, the role of the social science researcher as a presumptive spokesperson for others, that is as one who claims to make visible, (re)represent, and speak on behalf of others, must be critically examined.

PART II

Scales of provision and intermediaries

5. Shifting scales of infrastructure provision

Bas Van Vliet

INTRODUCTION

In 2001, the Dutch Ministries of Environment, Economic Affairs and Sciences decided to fund a five-year demonstration project proposal called Decentralized Sanitation and Reuse. The project was initiated by a group of environmental engineers who had denounced the existing sewerage system since the early 1970s as wasteful in water, energy and nutrients, and as being too centrally organized, inflexible and creating rigid and long-enduring dependency of users on big institutions. Instead the engineers have developed and promoted small-scale, simple sanitation techniques, based on the anaerobe treatment of concentrated (human) waste (Zeeman and Lettinga, 1999).

The funding by the Dutch government should not be interpreted as a major shift in policy-making on sewerage and sanitation. Centrally organized sewer systems are, and will remain, the dominant infrastructure to handle human waste. In fact the major trend is a further 'up-scaling' of sewer and treatment systems, using pressure pipes to lead urban waste water to the peri-urban large-scale treatment installations. Yet the current experimentation with decentralized sanitation is a unique opportunity to show the possible diversions from the 'beaten track' of sewer technology.

The call for decentralized technologies is nothing new. The environmental debate on the provision of infrastructure services, like water works and energy supply, has long been dominated by the controversy between advocates of small-scale decentralized technology on the one hand and defenders of large-scale networks on the other. Schumacher's 'Small is Beautiful' thesis was based on the assumption that human needs and the environment are better served by small-scale technologies and systems of management rather than large-scale technological systems. On the other hand defenders of large-scale provision claim that this is more efficient in not only economic but also environmental terms, and can also be better managed as it is based upon central organization.

Two issues emerge from this. The first is: what is small and what is large? Anyone who has been in the proximity of a modern wind turbine would be impressed by its size. Yet would the same wind turbine still be regarded as large in terms of electricity production and especially when compared to other electricity generators? There is no hard definition to give for 'small' and 'large' as they only have a meaning in comparison with other things. Even more complicating is the fact that apparently small technologies might only work in combination with huge technological networks. A car might be small compared to other modes of transport (planes, trains), but if we include the necessary infrastructure of roads and petrol stations in the definition of a car it is anything but a small-scale technology.

The second striking issue is that the brief sketch of the dichotomy between small- and large-scale provision of infrastructure services shows that the debate refers not only to (the scale of) technology but also to (the scale of) its social organization. There is of course nothing new in the idea that technological change can only be analysed if its social organization is included in such a study. However, it seems that the discussion of optimal scales of energy, water and other network-bound systems rarely diverges from technological parameters and, if it does, scale of technologies is too easily matched with a similar scale of social organization.

This chapter argues that contemporary environmental renewal in networks of water, waste and energy service provision at least challenges these links between scale of technology and scale of management and use. It is demonstrated that the labels 'monopolist provider' and 'captive consumer' no longer suffice to describe the more complicated social relations within network-bound provision of environmentally relevant services. A better insight into these relations may help utility managers, policy-makers and consumers to rethink their position towards the network-bound systems that provide the major inputs for everyday life. Utility managers may diversify products and services so as to serve specific consumer groups. Policy-makers may renew their policy frameworks to allow utilities to modernize infrastructures as well as their modes of provision. Consumers may benefit by demanding tailor-made services from the utilities instead of uniform products.

Section 2 discusses the main triggers for differentiation of network-bound systems: the wide spread liberalization of utility markets, demand-side management and the need for more sustainable production and consumption of energy, water and waste services. As 'scale' is too generic a term, the third section distinguishes four dimensions of scale that might help to analyse aspects of socio-technical differentiation within network-bound systems. To illustrate the relevance of distinguishing such socio-technical dimensions, two cases are presented: the first a sustainable housing project in which the residents experimented with 'down-scaled' water technologies; the second a project of solar electricity generation on the roofs of one of the largest new-built residential areas in the Netherlands. Section 4 discusses the implications of different scales of organization for the roles and responsibilities of both providers and consumers of energy, water and waste services. In conclusion it is argued that it is time to abandon the dichotomy between 'small' and 'large' in network-bound service provision, and replace it with concepts that more appropriately reflect the differentiated social and technical relations in these systems of provision and consumption.

TRIGGERS FOR DIFFERENTIATION

The provision of drinking water, sewerage services, electricity and gas to European households has been established through mainly large-scale networks benefiting from a natural monopoly and economies of scale. Natural monopolies are market situations in which network providers are the only providers in a region, because there is only one network available. They are termed 'natural' because competition between different parallel networks in one region would be economically inefficient for all parties. The term 'economies of scale' refers to the fact that some sorts of provision are only beneficial if there is a minimum number of users or clients, or a minimum size of a network.

Around 1900, most urban infrastructures across Europe were provided by private companies. Many gas and electricity networks, piped water systems and even roads and railways started as local networks, connecting a handful of wealthy clients within one region of manageable size. Once established, the large-scale investments that were needed to extend the networks to connect all households, including remote ones, could not be handled by private parties alone. Therefore state provision of these services became the dominant mode of provision from the beginning of the twentieth century onwards. Until the early 1980s, water, electricity, gas, sewage and waste service provision could thus be characterized as publicly managed large-scale provision.

Contemporary socio-technological innovations in urban infrastructures in the Netherlands and other northern EU member states seem to have triggered differentiation in scales of provision. New technologies in water provision range from large-scale dual networks supplying drinking water and 'use' water (water for general use but not for drinking and personal hygiene), to community-level rainwater retention systems and in-house rainwater tanks. Energy-related environmental innovations can encompass small and large techniques of generation and distribution: from solar panels on the roofs of individual houses, to combined heat and power (CHP) generation plants at district level up to proposals to install offshore wind parks in the North Sea or mega solar plants (Truffer et al., 2002).

Such processes of differentiation can in a large part be attributed to the liberalization of utility markets and the privatization of utility networks. Both have triggered a process of spatial, institutional and technological 'splintering' in the delivery of utility-based products and services and the development and management of utility networks (Graham and Marvin, 1995). 'Splintering' refers not only to the differentiation of services and products offered by utilities, but also to the fragmentation of utility services and management practices as they become implemented at a range of different scales.

Apart from the liberalization of utility markets there are at least two other parallel developments which have contributed to the emerging divergence of scales: demand-side management as a way to cope with resource and capacity problems, and the increasing utilization of renewable resources (Van Vliet, 2002). Demand-side management approaches, which emerged in the late 1970s as a solution to resource scarcity or to put ceilings on network capacity, included the down-scaling of measurements from system level to solutions applied at the level of end-consumers. Instead of expanding resource extraction and infrastructure capacity to meet increasing demand, the new approach was to minimize demand so as to make better use of existing capacities (Gellings, 1996). Technologies that were put in place included night storage heaters to limit peak demand, efficiency devices such as low-energy light bulbs and low flush-toilet cisterns – all representing typically down-scaled solutions for large-scale problems.

The third development is the utilization of renewable resources such as the sun and wind for energy, lake water for drinking water and renewable techniques for waste treatment such as composting. Most of these technologies are applied and used at a local level, although larger-scale application is not excluded. Smaller-scale electricity-generating technologies such as CHP plants and solar panels can partly replace large-scale power plants. The same can be said of rainwater and grey-water systems which can partly replace large-scale water works. Community composting and private garden composting bins may make landfilling or incineration of biowaste obsolete. These possibilities for small-scale applications distinguish renewable resources from conventional ones. Fossil fuels and nuclear resources for energy, reservoirs for water supply, or incineration plants and landfilling sites for waste, all inherently require large-scale application to benefit from economies of scale. The emergence of renewables in all three sectors, and their promising future, will contribute to the further diversification of scales of application of energy, water and waste technologies.

FOUR DIMENSIONS OF SCALE IN UTILITY SERVICES

If it were only the scale of applied technologies that changes, nothing much essential would have changed in network-bound systems. The services would still be provided by mostly state-owned organizations, owners of the physical networks in the region and monopolists in service provision. Consumers would still be anonymous users, charged with fixed rates or taxes for the services provided. However, the diversification in scales of the 'hardware' goes hand in hand with a diversification of the 'software': the practices of consumers, providers and their mutual relations. Different small and large providers have a wider range of roles to play in the provision of services than was formerly possible. In many cases consumers may now decide to switch between providers and choose between a differentiated palette of services.

In the case of smaller-scale technologies, that are applied at the level of the household, one might assume that consumers will be more involved in how utility resources are supplied to them. However, diversification of scales of technology does not automatically imply parallel diversification in terms of management or ownership. Indeed most of the large-scale technological innovations, such as biomass power plants, are operated by utility companies, while small-scale innovations such as low-flow cistern devices and energy-efficient light bulbs are most often installed and used by individual consumers. However, some inverse relations between technological scales and the organization of management and ownership are also possible. Provision through large-scale networks might be 'splintered' into distributed generation and more autonomy on the local level, while the organization of the whole system might at the same time be even more up-scaled. Thus apart from being highly relative terms, scale and size may refer to different technical and social dimensions. Four such dimensions can be distinguished: technical scale, scale of management, reach of a system, and whether technologies can be applied on a stand-alone or a grid-connected basis.

Scale of Technology

This is the most common understanding of 'scale' and just refers to the size of the artefacts involved. Small scale solutions for environmental problems that replace large-scale technologies include the composting toilet, the solar cooker, human-powered lamps and radios and so forth. 'Small-scale' usually refers to the size of the artefact or to its use on a local level, and in many cases to both. Small is considered even more 'beautiful' if it is also 'simple', which is often characterized by a technology that is easily constructed from local materials and can be maintained without the help of highly qualified technicians. In the environmental debate nuclear power stations, oil refineries, wastewater treatment plants, landfills, intensive cattle breeding and many other industrial activities are generally considered large-scale technologies.

Scale of Management

The degree to which the scale of technology does not always match the scale of management can be observed in high-tech innovations in energy and water infrastructures. A small-scale energy generation unit such as micro-CHP or a system of on-site anaerobic treatment of wastewater is often managed and maintained not by individual consumers but by the larger expertise organizations that installed these units in the first place. By agreeing leases and contracts with service companies, users of those small-scale units assure themselves of the trouble-free functioning of these systems. Apart from the fact that the generation or treatment units are of a smaller scale, the management of these systems is similar to that of large-scale utility systems.

An example of the opposite situation (large-scale technology with small-scale management organization) is the exploitation and management of a wind turbine or wind park by one or more owners and users. All over Europe there are windmill owners (individuals and associations) who sell their excess capacity to energy utility companies.

Not only can the number of actors or size of organization involved be an indicator of the scale of management, so too can the level of expertise needed to run a system. In some cases lay knowledge may be sufficient (as in the case of how to maintain a solar panel); in other cases expert knowledge is required to keep a system running (micro-CHP).

The Reach of a Technology

Artefacts may be small but they might be used in such volumes that their reach is large or extensive. A normal bicycle is a small-scale device in several aspects: it is a stand-alone artefact, used and maintained locally, and generally does not need much expertise or knowledge to run. However, in the case of the Netherlands, it is used by millions of people as a day-to-day means of (urban) transport. In this respect the reach of the bicycle is far from small scale. The massive use of bikes has also triggered the building of urban infrastructures like bicycle lanes and stands, repair shops, road signs and long-distance cycling routes. In a different case, should composting toilets ever become a success it would require the development of large-scale infrastructures of compost collection, handling and reuse.

Stand-alone Versus Fully Grid-Connected

A related issue that further complicates the conceptualization of technological scale is whether a small-scale artefact can function as a stand-alone device or only performs if it is connected to a larger socio-technical infrastructure. A bicycle can be a stand-alone technology as one can still ride a bicycle in the absence of bicycle lanes. A wind-up radio may be a stand-alone device in terms of its energy use, but without the ether network of radio frequencies it would be of no use at all. Solar panels are good examples of technologies that can be used both off- and on-grid.

To summarize: debates around scales of technology and especially the social expectations that come along with them, would be more useful if reference were made to the different dimensions of scale. In relation to the liberalization of utility markets this is especially important as the conventional dichotomy between small (supposedly being beautiful or environmentally sound) and large (supposedly being economically efficient) does not suffice. This is particularly the case given that processes of liberalization have triggered socio-technical differentiation and the creation of niche markets of local or green utility services provision with mixed scales of technology or management. The implications of such differentiated scales of provision for the relations between providers and consumers of energy, water and waste services are illustrated by two cases of environmental innovation in which one or more dimensions of scale have been altered, as compared to conventional systems of provision.

Small-Scale Waterworks in a Sustainable Homes Project

The first example is Het Groene Dak, a Dutch ecological housing project of 60 homes initiated in 1991. As well as incorporating several, at that time radical, methods of insulation and material use, the most innovative measures were those taken to minimize the consumption of tap water, in two shared apartment blocks (Chappells et al., 2000). The residents of these blocks had managed to realize most of their initial social and environmental objectives, including high standards of sustainability (renewable building materials, non-toxic paints, high insulation measures, low water use devices, solar heating and so forth), as well as independence from large-scale centralized water supply and sewerage systems, as far as was possible within existing technological and legislative boundaries. To become more independent of central systems of water supply and wastewater management, residents were successful in their lobby to the housing corporation and local water company to have installed a rainwater collection and distribution system to supply water to washing machines; composting toilets that do not use any water for flushing or require a connection to the sewer; and a grey-water tank, reed-bed filter and retention pond for all other wastewater treatment. It is clear that this is a case of the down-scaling of water provision technology and that down-scaling occurs in several dimensions.

First, with stand-alone toilets and the on-site generation of water and treatment of wastewater, the technology of waterworks is scaled down to the household level compared to conventional water supply and sewerage. Only the supply of water for drinking is left to a large network provider: the local water company.

Second, residents had responsibility for the daily management and maintenance of the installed technology. The composting toilets needed much maintenance, especially compared to normal flush toilets, and the composting process was to be monitored carefully. Residents learned that it was a rather uncontrollable process, but installed new ventilation, drainage and other devices to improve it. The remaining sludge needed to be dug out from the tank and reused in their garden or disposed of in other ways. The rainwater recovery system worked without any problems. Distinct from 'normal' drinking water supply, rainwater is collected, distributed and used in the one location. Residents are therefore not only consumers, but also their own water providers.

A third dimension of scale is the societal reach of technologies. The project was one of only a few sustainable housing projects located in the midst of conventional housing areas at the time, and its impact on the world of centralized water works was marginal. However, it was deliberately set up as an exemplar project: the initiators wanted to learn from their experiences and extend it to future initiatives. Their experiences were systematically listed on a website, including detailed tables of water quality indicators, and water and electricity consumption levels (www.groenedak.nl). Also the continuing story of maintenance problems in the case of the composting toilets was well covered. The project became infamous when the residents decided to get rid of the composting toilets after seven years of failure. Much to the annoyance of the project initiators, they found that due to the possible risk of explosion of, or contamination by, accumulated gases within the composting tanks, only professionals wearing protective clothing and gas masks could do the demolition. The picture of white-suited and gas-masked professionals breaking down a supposedly 'eco-friendly' toilet was published in national newspapers and achieved national TV coverage. In terms of reach, the composting toilets had much more impact than only on their users. Since the public failure of the system in Groene Dak, compost toilets seem to have vanished from the sustainable building agenda in the Netherlands.

The fourth and last dimension of scale refers to how and to what extent technologies are connected to larger-scale infrastructures or grids. The initiators of the Groene Dak project were eager to become as independent and self-sufficient as possible in terms of water use. At first sight, the rainwater system and composting toilets are indeed stand-alone devices as no grid connections are needed. However, drinking water is still supplied in the conventional way and may also be needed for back-up provision in times of drought or in case of technical failure. As the composting toilets did not produce reusable compost, the remaining sludge had to be disposed of through the municipal biowaste collection and treatment chain. Avoiding the use of a sewer system essentially transferred the burden to the biowaste collection system. In environmental terms this might be a better option, but in terms of being self-sufficient and independent of large infrastructures this is not necessarily the case. The residents of Groene Dak have experienced that in urban housing projects it proves very difficult, if not impossible, to avoid connection to larger infrastructures.

Solar Panels in a Variety of Grid Connections

A second example of different scales of socio-technical organization concerns the application of solar (photovoltaic) panels for electricity generation. Solar panels are small electricity generators that can be applied at several scales: from stand-alone appliances as in the case of beacons, to grid-connected solar power stations in which thousands of panels may be linked together. In terms of ownership and management arrangements the variety is almost endless. In Amersfoort (the Netherlands) the regional energy company is the owner of thousands of solar panels that are installed on the roofs of new-built houses (the 1 MegaWatt project, as described in Chappells et al., 2000). The generated electricity is either transferred to the central grid (and delivered to all clients in the region) or directly delivered to the householders living underneath the solar roofs. Other arrangements comprise a set of solar panels that can be purchased from the energy company and installed on individual roofs. The generated electricity is used in the household, while the excess can be 'sold' to the energy provider by configuring the meter to run forward or backward according to levels of sunshine and domestic consumption (net-metering).

As for the socio-political reach of solar panels, most developments (including the Amersfoort project) depend on local, national or European subsidy programmes because the electricity generated remains more expensive than that generated by other sources. The share of solar energy in the contemporary green electricity market is therefore marginal compared to, for instance, biomass and waste-to-energy conversion. However, solar power has, compared to other 'green' sources, an almost unblemished record when it comes to disputes about its environmental soundness. Contrary to biomass-based electricity production, there is no greenhouse gas emission in the conversion of sunlight into electricity, and unlike wind turbines there is hardly any problem of siting or landscape pollution. Moreover having a solar panel on one's roof does much more for the green image of a household than participation in green electricity schemes. Such symbolic attractiveness of solar energy helps to enhance the reach of the technology, for its reach would be negligible if only economic considerations were taken into account.[1]

Solar panels are typically flexible when it comes to grid connection, the fourth dimension of scale. When used on a stand-alone basis, mostly with a battery for energy storage, solar panels are distributed as 'solar kits'. For example donor projects provide a framework to establish electricity supply in the rural areas of developing countries. Real stand-alone appliances are however rarely the case. Although there are no electricity lines to connect to, the user will be dependent on proper battery maintenance and supply of spare parts by third parties.[2]

Most solar panel applications, especially in the less sunnier areas like Britain and the Netherlands, do need a connection to the electricity grid for back-up. Excess electricity produced on long sunny days can then be delivered to the central grid, while all the other days can still be comfortable thanks to electricity supply from the grid. Such small generators dispersed over the network can only be described as a distributed generation of electricity. The network no longer accommodates only a one-way supply of electricity from central power station to individual consumers, but a two-way road of supply and demand based on dispersed electricity generation and consumption.

The micro-power revolution as foreseen by Dunn (2000), among others, places great emphasis on solar panels and other environmentally sound innovations that need to be run on a smaller scale than the contemporary central power plants. Different from the Schumacher school that strives for self-sufficiency, micro-power presupposes a large-scale network to accommodate the two-way road of supply and demand. In such a new constellation, the categories 'small' and 'large' no longer suffice because the energy, water and waste networks combine small and large in several new ways which makes it impossible to draw a clear line between small- and large-scale applications. To summarize and visualize the differentiation of scales, Figure 5.1 shows six of the technologies that are mentioned in the text plotted on the four dimensions of scale that were outlined in section 3. Distinguishing small from large in terms of size (the first dimension) might be relatively easy, but for other dimensions apparently similar technologies appear to be quite different from each other.

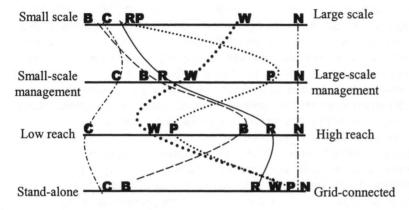

C: Composting toilet
P: Photovoltaic panel (1 MW project)
B: Bicycle
R: Radio
W: Wind turbine
N: Nuclear power plant

Figure 5.1 Six technologies mentioned in the text and their scale dimensions

ROLES AND RESPONSIBILITIES OF CONSUMERS AND PROVIDERS IN DISTRIBUTED UTILITY SERVICE PROVISION

If the dichotomy between small and large scale no longer suffices, what can be said about the roles of providers and consumers in new constellations of distributed energy, water or waste provision? Two examples of small-scale waterworks and solar panels help address this question.

As indicated, the Groene Dak project was set up as an exemplar project and for that reason residents put much effort into monitoring and publishing data concerning the use of the various new technologies and materials. An illustration of this reflective approach is given by a resident who was the main initiator of the water-saving technologies in the project. After some years of usage and experimentation he came to the conclusion that in terms of environmental impacts related to water consumption, it is best to rely on supply from a centralized water provider. Although the rainwater collection system worked very well, it was based on an electric pump system that distributed water from the basement to the attic. The compost toilets may have saved a lot of water, but they also consumed a lot of electricity due to the drainage and ventilation systems that were installed in attempts to improve the composting process. A comparison of the measured kilowatt hours used per saved cubic metre of water and the energy use of a cubic metre of conventional drinking water supply, showed that the latter is much more energy efficient (twice as efficient in the case of the rainwater system and as much as 20 times more in the case of composting toilets; Post, 2000). The initiator concluded that on environmental grounds it is inefficient to rely on the alternative water systems that were applied in Groene Dak.

Although this story provides only anecdotal evidence, it demonstrates how highly committed consumers of utility services have attempted to redefine their position towards conventional providers and systems of provision. As the case of solar panels and green electricity also illustrated, less 'active' or more 'ordinary' consumers might also find themselves wondering if, how and to what extent electricity should be produced and delivered from centralized or decentralized sources, and who should be responsible for producing it (including the option of being a self-provider).

The 1 MegaWatt project in Amersfoort is designed not only to experiment with photovoltaic technology, but with various kinds of ownership and client–provider relations in energy provision as well. To allow investigation of effects of the various forms of ownership and management, half of the installations are owned by the local energy company. Agreements have been made with the developers concerned, which include accessibility of the installations and liability for any damage. A right of superficies (building right) has been established in respect of the plots. It has also been stipulated that the solar panels should remain unshaded (which restricts the planting of large trees in front of one's home). The residents are remunerated by the energy company for the exploitation of their roofs. Twenty per cent of the energy generated on their roof will be paid for at the normal domestic consumer tariff.

The other half of the solar power installations in Amersfoort have become the property of residents. The solar power generated is fed into the mains grid and in return residents receive the normal domestic user tariff. After evaluating the project, the energy company has stated that it does not intend to implement the scheme elsewhere. Managers suggest that too much expertise was required for roof construction, which is not the core business of an energy company (interview REMU, 1999, in Chappells et al., 2000).

Processes of diversification of scale are likely to continue in the electricity sector, as electricity is a flexible, easily transportable form of energy provision. With co-generators like photovoltaic panels on consumers' roofs, the electricity grid is partly transferred into a storage system of redundant electricity that is produced at the household level.

CONCLUSIONS

Different scales of socio-technical organization and moves towards distributed generation are associated with changing relations between the consumers and providers of utility services, but not in easily definable ways. Understanding these changes requires a closer reading of forms of differentiation – seen through the different technical, institutional, organizational and social arrangements along national, local and household grids. Consumers might become more authoritative in certain areas, while others remain captive consumers as the schemes range from possibilities for self-provision on the one hand, to compelled consumption of centrally provided services on the other.

Differentiation in network-bound systems, which takes many forms including the differentiation in scale, has enabled a diversification of consumer roles towards the provision of network-bound services (see also Van Vliet, 2002, 2003). From an anonymous captive user, consumer roles have diversified into that of being a 'normal' consumer who can choose between different market options; a citizen-consumer who links consumption with societal issues (green electricity, fair trade); and even a co-provider, who not only uses centrally provided water, electricity or waste services but also produces them on his or her own premises (solar electricity, rainwater, waste composting). Combinations of these roles are also possible, as we have seen in the case of Groene Dak.

Of course one has to be cautious about the impact such arrangements have in terms of room for manoeuvre for consumers and the greening of network-bound provision and consumption. Whether liberalization has really brought free choice for consumers, as promised in the marketing campaigns accompanying liberalization processes, can be disputed. Summerton (this volume) has shown that in the case of Californian and Swedish electricity sectors, instead of offering consumers the choice between providers, liberalization has enabled utilities to choose their consumers.

Likewise the assumption that the application of on-site technologies, or distributed generation in general, means that consumers gain power towards service providers should be critically assessed. Whether consumers gain power over how or which network-bound services are provided depends on more than the size of technology or the scale of its application.

In analysing contemporary technology development in infrastructures of consumption, the use of a simple dichotomy of small-scale technology (supposedly being beautiful, environmentally sound and socially acceptable) versus large-scale technology (supposedly being economical, environmentally damaging and creating social inequalities) should therefore be abandoned. 'Small' and 'large' become fluid terms if one considers the contemporary technological innovations that have been triggered by liberalization of utility networks, demand-side management and sustainability strategies. The trend towards decentralizing generation with the application of smaller-scale generation technologies is counterweighted by the parallel trend of ever-increasing networks which connect all small generation technologies to each other (and are centrally controlled). It is not the scale of technology that moulds the social relations between providers and consumers, but rather the management of networks. As a consequence the relations between service providers and consumers should no longer be defined in terms of a rhetoric of 'large-scale production' and 'small-scale consumption' or 'top-down provision', but by 'distributed generation', 'interaction' and 'co-provision'.

The Decentralized Sanitation and Reuse project might gain much more impact in the world of sewerage and waste management if small scale is not proposed as a social and technological panacea, but if environmental engineers find ways to incorporate multiple scales of innovation within the social and technological context of existing infrastructures of water supply, waste management and sewerage provision.

NOTES

1. Solar panels are highly expensive as long as they are produced and applied on a marginal scale. Mass application would however lower the costs per Watt Peak. The cost of solar electricity has gone down from 6.26 euros per Watt Peak in April 2002 to 5.97 euros in October 2003 (www.solarbuzz.com/moduleprices.htm).
2. And this represents the weakest aspect of these projects.

6. Sustainable infrastructures by proxy? Intermediation beyond the production–consumption nexus

Simon Marvin and Will Medd

INTRODUCTION

In February 2003 the UK Environment Secretary Margaret Beckett announced the development of a national strategy for 'sustainable consumption and production', meeting the commitment made at the Johannesburg Summit.[1] The announcement closely resonated with existing programmes such as Agenda 21 that identified the major cause of deterioration in the global environment as 'unsustainable patterns of consumption and production' (Chapter 4) that, according to the Rio Declaration, member states should seek to 'reduce and eliminate' (Principle 8) (see Blaza et al., 2002).

Consistent across these strategies is a commitment to achieving sustainability through reshaped and revised patterns of production and consumption. Each strategy generates a clear distinction between two spheres of activity – namely the production of goods, products and services in one sphere, and their consumption and use in another sphere. Sustainability objectives must then address two sets of social interests, producers and consumers, to reshape their practices and technologies to lower demand for services and reduce the impacts of production. Key assumptions underlie these objectives: that there is a distance between production and consumption spheres; that the interests of production and consumption are discrete; and that they can each be subject to relevant policy measures to reduce and eliminate unsustainable patterns of resource use. Yet this binary divide implicit in contemporary policy ignores the intervening linkages between production and consumption. What fills the gap between production and consumption? Where are the boundaries at which production and consumption meet? How can production and consumption be mutually reshaped?

While policy programmes currently work to address the largely separate spheres of production and consumption, in this chapter we argue that in relation to infrastructural dynamics there is a need to start addressing the 'intermediary' space between production and consumption.[2] This intermediary space is a context where the apparently firm boundaries between production and consumption can be questioned, broken down, reworked and actively reconstructed by intermediaries that cannot simply be understood as representing the interests or practices of either producers or consumers. The concept of 'intermediaries' is used to capture the characteristics of new organizations and social–technical configurations that lie outside the formal infrastructure and yet which strategically mediate between sets of different social interests and infrastructural dynamics, creating new intermediary spaces in which notions of sustainable action are being played out.

The conceptualization of new intermediaries is situated within the context of wider shifts in the social organization of infrastructure networks and here we take as our focus the water sector. Networked infrastructures are a particularly useful window into the emergence of intermediaries and intermediary action. Under monopoly conditions networks have been understood as a simple producer–consumer relationship, with a single provider supplying an undifferentiated product to mass consumers. Distribution networks act as the technical linkages between production and consumption interests. Consequently the wider implications of recent transformations in the social organization of the water sector can be traced through the changing relations between production and consumption interests (see for example Marvin and Guy, 1997; Graham and Marvin, 2001). Key here is the way that processes of privatization, liberalization and regulation of the water sector have transformed the relations between production and consumption interests and the ways in which new contexts for intermediary action have been created.

The chapter highlights how infrastructural transition (Guy et al., 2001) is supporting the emergence of new intermediaries that take a variety of social, technical and networked forms, and can reshape the traditional relations between supply and use. There are many examples of intermediaries including websites through which particular configurations of suppliers can be linked to differentiated consumer requirements; advice and consultancy agencies that show the benefits of sustainable water management for business users; and organizations linking low-income groups to sustainable technologies for low-cost homes. Such activities involve a wide range of organizations such as commercial enterprises, consultants, non-profit-making organizations and campaigning groups. Intermediaries may enable the introduction of new technologies, provide education about sustainable practices or support the coming together of a diverse range of interests for joint action in shaping the water environment. In this chapter we take just three examples for illustrative purposes, namely housing associations, business advice and promotional activities.

A note of caution: these new intermediaries are not always successful or necessarily inherently positive for either the environment or all users. For example intermediaries tend to be highly selective and may focus on premium users who are offered additional services and savings, while low-income or small users may not be so attractive to intermediaries driven by a commercial logic. Although intermediaries may actively promote resource-saving practices and activities to reduce the costs of utility services to large users, they can also help stimulate additional demands for utility services by lowering costs of service or promoting technologies, such as power showers, that drive up demand. Intermediary action is not therefore inevitably resource-saving. Consequently it is necessary to highlight the presence and role of particular logics of intermediary action that are increasingly significant within the context of infrastructural change. These new intermediary logics need to be taken seriously by research and policy with a view to exploring further what the implications for sustainability might be.

The chapter is set out as follows. First we begin with a brief account of the transformation of water infrastructures in which unbundling has led to the proliferation of 'intermediaries'. Second, we introduce three illustrative examples of 'new intermediaries', describing the different and hybrid forms they take. Third, we highlight key aspects of the new intermediaries, namely their selectivity, situatedness and valorization. Fourth, we examine the notion of the role of intermediaries in generating 'sustainability by proxy'. Finally, we conclude with suggestions on the research and policy challenges of intermediary activity.

TRANSFORMING INFRASTRUCTURE: THE EMERGENCE OF INTERMEDIARIES

Transformations in the social organization of infrastructural provision create a new context that has stimulated the development of intermediaries within an enlarged space (real or conceptual space) between production and consumption. More specifically, intermediaries bring together new technologies and changed social practices that offer important possibilities for reshaping the relations between production and consumption. But what are intermediaries?

If we take intermediaries as people and objects that act 'in between' different processes, then everything can be considered an intermediary. For example we could consider the intermediaries that enable water to reach domestic taps, from the tap itself through to watersheds and reservoirs, and the complex of pipes, laboratories, institutions and people in between. In other words, assemblages of technological, social and hydrological intermediaries combine at various points to form the water cycle. Indeed we could trace the 'biography' of water to explore the role of intermediaries throughout its history, from 'the first flood' to the 'water wars' (Ball, 1999). An enlarged approach to intermediaries builds awareness of the significant role that a variety of phenomena play in the production and consumption of an apparently simple resource. This view focuses attention on the heterogeneity of infrastructural provision and to the importance of 'heterogeneous engineers' in creating the complex assemblages we call water infrastructure (Latour, 1996; Law, 1987). But if everything that sits between a supplier and a user is an intermediary what is the explanatory value of the concept?

In its everyday use the term 'intermediary' tends to have a more specific meaning that incorporates the intentionality of the intermediary. Intermediaries are deliberately positioned to act in between by bringing together and mediating between different interests. There are for instance spiritual intermediaries, financial intermediaries, health intermediaries, peacekeeping intermediaries and web-based intermediaries. These intermediaries position themselves to have a particular role in literally intermediating between sets of different social interests, to produce an outcome that would not have been possible, or as effective, without their involvement. An intermediary is not necessarily either a producer or consumer but they may well work between these interests to achieve an objective. Such intermediaries are, then, strategic.

Bringing the discussion back to water we can argue that under classic monopoly conditions water networks were configured around a powerful supply logic designed to provide clean water to domestic users to ensure wider public health, and to industry to support economic development. The logic were to ensure that the production and use of water was uninterrupted so that there was no need for intermediaries to intervene between producers and users unless they accelerated the provision of water. Water supply passed through a complex range of social, natural and technical intermediaries and these were assembled to narrow the gap between production and consumption interests to ensure the rapid, reliable and continuous flow of water to users. Domestic water metering, for instance, has been rare in the UK because of the desire to guarantee that water was not restricted in households and to ensure collective public health. Only at times of water shortage was the relationship between supply and use brought into view and subject to scrutiny as public water providers exhorted users to temporarily reduce demand during a drought, before re-establishing normal relations.

Hence while traditional actors such as consultants or public health professionals might be considered as intermediaries, 'new intermediaries' emerged in the water sector when the context of producer–consumer relations changed. Organizing infrastructure under classic monopoly conditions meant that the distance between production and consumption interests was deliberately short, as the public producer of water was responsible for assembling the complex socio-technical–natural relations required to deliver water to mass markets. Public health intermediaries had a role in ensuring that households used water to ensure cleanliness and disease prevention. Users were assigned a relatively passive role that was to consume sufficient clean water to ensure that wider public health conditions were met. Within the context of privatization in 1989, there have been shifts in the social organization and priorities of the water sector that have significantly reshaped the relations between production and consumption interests, creating an enlarged context for intermediaries and intermediation. The key to understanding this context is the dual process of the unbundling of integrated infrastructure networks and their selective rebundling by intermediaries (see Graham and Marvin, 2001).

Commercialization, privatization and liberalization of networked infrastructure effectively unbundled an integrated network into competitive and monopolistic segments. There has been separation of roles vertically and horizontally, of spatial areas through which services are delivered, and of types of consumers whom the market-oriented companies target. At the same time new concerns have arisen around particular consumer interests, regulation and sustainability that, coupled with processes of fragmentation, have consequences for the coordination of consumption and provision. It is within the space of infrastructural fragmentation that new possibilities for the role of intermediaries are emerging. These 'intermediaries' are deliberately positioned to have mediating roles in relation to sustainability.

THE WORK OF INTERMEDIARIES: TOILETS, HOUSES AND BUSINESS

Within the context of infrastructural transformation we are interested in the emergence of strategic intermediaries that have a role in reshaping production and consumption practices. This section introduces three examples of intermediary activity and highlights how they work across a range of interests that do not neatly fit within either the 'production' or 'consumption' spheres. These intermediaries always appear in hybrid forms, combining technology, organizations and networks as well as texts, money and people (see Callon, 1997), and constitute new forms of interdependencies and socio-technical assemblages, as with infrastructure itself (Graham and Marvin, 2001, pp. 30–31). As such the legitimacy and expertise of intermediaries do not emerge within a space between distinct spheres of production and consumption, but gain their legitimacy by working across the boundaries of a range of interests not normally considered as significant to strategies of sustainability. The following examples demonstrate the particularities of intermediary activity.

Example 1: Toilets – 'Save-a-Flush'

There are very simple technologies that can be placed in the toilet cistern to reduce the amount of water used when a toilet is flushed. During droughts for example, people in the UK were encouraged to put bricks in the cistern to reduce the water used for flushing. More recently companies have developed various devices that are easier to store, distribute and to fit (without damaging the cistern) than a brick. For example 'Save-a-flush' is a 'simple, proven and effective means of making substantial savings on water usage' and is estimated to reduce water usage by around 1 litre for every flush. Various brands have now been developed including 'the hog', 'the hippo' and the 'soggy doggy'.

This simple technology however has not been easy to introduce and there have been various campaigns to generate wider uptake. The website of the save-a-flush supplier emphasizes the specific benefits for households, businesses and hospitals.[3] The UK Department of the Environment, Transport and the Regions (DETR) campaign 'Are You Doing Your Bit?' features the fitting of save-a-flush devices (branded as the 'hog') as part of its approach to encourage 'small but important behavioural changes in our everyday actions to benefit both ourselves and the local and global environment'.[4] Water companies have also been encouraged by the UK Office of Water Services (OFWAT) to make cistern devices available free of charge upon request. Some for example have linked this to promoting 'self-audit' activity by households and in some cases schools have been used to develop a context for introducing such devices.

The save-a-flush device 'sits quietly in the cistern'. And yet it cannot be located simply within the domain of production and consumption. For water utilities save-a-flush can reduce water consumption that, in a context where water metering for individual households is not in place, is a saving for the company. For businesses and hospitals as consumers with different metering arrangements save-a-flush can also offer commercial advantage, by reducing unnecessary costs. And yet through the promotional campaigns save-a-flush also reaches other interests. For example it can contribute to local authorities' desire to gain 'Green Organization' status. In the case of 'Are You Doing Your Bit?' it is claimed to contribute to reducing the amount of water taken from rivers and boreholes. The intermediaries promoting the save-a-flush devices enrol a range of interests through networks of relationships between government programmes, water company targets, schools and users that span the interests of both production and consumption. The extent to which it is successful is disputed, of course. Of particular note is the question of whether people resort to flushing the toilet a second or third time.

Example 2: Social Housing and Water Recycling

Housing associations have been exploring ways in which new developments can contribute to keeping costs down for low-income tenants. One example is in Liverpool where the Harlow Park Housing Co-operation, in partnership with CDS Housing Association, has developed 33 houses in Toxteth.[5] The scheme was initiated when council tenants in run-down accommodation campaigned for better housing within their community. The housing association offered support and sought to build housing that would have low environmental impact, thus reinforcing the case for planning permission and offering cheaper running costs for low-income households. The specification included: grey-water recycling (in four houses, sponsored by North West Water); low-flush six-litre WCs; spray taps and showers over baths; and water butts.

Difficulties were encountered with the grey-water recycling. Two different types of recycling devices were tried. One required the tenants to undertake manual introduction of treatment fluid. It was not known if the tenants kept this up. An alternative was a computer system that would introduce the treatment automatically and so would not require the tenants to do anything. This system however had difficulties because of grit in the system (from the water tanks), which would clog it up (the company supplying this subsequently went out of business). Both systems involved a switch to the mains if there was not enough water or if treatment was not undertaken (it is possible for residents to leave the system switched to mains). Engineers in the scheme also suggested that because of the other water-saving devices in the houses (for example spray taps and showers) the water flow was relatively low which limited the effectiveness and efficiency of the grey-water system. CDS has not repeated the grey-water recycling in other developments and has instead concentrated on water butts, showers, low-flush toilets and low-flow taps.

The Housing Association emerges as an intermediary within the water sector in the space between the consumer (tenants) and the producer (water company). Although the housing association has always played a role in mediating between the needs of tenants, in the context of infrastructural unbundling they are forming a new intermediary role strategically situated between different interests (low-income households, promotional opportunities of a water company and the concerns of planners) to situate the new technology within the homes. The logics of production and consumption are again problematized. The same technology bridges the different interests through the active intermediary work of the housing association. Here then the housing association uses its expertise to negotiate from outside the traditional production–consumption nexus to instigate the introduction of water-saving devices.

Example 3: Advising Business – SWEL, Beds and SuDS

Sustainable Water Environment in Lancashire (SWEL) is an organization developed to offer advice and support to business in Lancashire. SWEL is funded through a partnership that involves the Groundwork Trust and the Environment Agency in North West England, and is funded through sources such as the European Regional Development Fund (ERDF) and the Sustainable Regeneration Budget (SRB). SWEL aims to offer advice and support to companies 'who wish to recognise and take advantage of significant business benefits available'. For a small fee, SWEL offers a range of support, such as audit, minimization advice, training, monitoring, targeting, on-site consultation and guidance.

SWEL offers numerous case studies of where its support has saved business financial costs by introducing more sustainable water practices. One case study is of a Silent Night Beds factory. SWEL has supported the factory in gaining a grant to implement a Sustainable Drainage System (SuDS) to deal with problems of flooding experienced by the factory. Not only did this reduce flooding but the development of SuDS is also seen to reduce flood flows and pollution in rivers.

In contrast to the promotion of save-a-flush by housing associations, the establishment of SWEL was explicitly to have an intermediary role within the water sector. It was motivated by the UK Environment Agency's (EA's) concern that it could not effectively be a regulator and an advisor at the same time. The EA established a pilot project, the forerunner of SWEL, to explore the possibility of an intermediary role. SWEL is able to work with companies in Lancashire to enable them to make commercial savings that meet the requirements of the EA and in turn benefit the water sector by reducing pollution. SWEL gains its legitimacy through its expertise in water-saving advice, but also through being able to work across and in between the different interests of the regulator and the business consumers.

REBUNDLING PRODUCTION–CONSUMPTION BOUNDARIES

As our examples show, intermediaries reconnect processes of production and consumption into new circuits of 'production–consumption'. Flushing the toilet with a 'save-a-flush' device is simultaneously a performance of reduced consumption of water and decreased production of wastewater. In this respect the device can be considered an intermediary that reintroduces a moment of reduced water production into the home. In the case of the new houses of the housing association, water-saving devices also work to produce less water in the moment of consumption, that also produces less wastewater. Some of the wastewater that is re-produced through recycling technologies again reduces the 'first class' water produced. In effect the houses become sites of production–consumption, not just sites of consumption. And in the case of the bed company, the development of SuDS involved the production of new forms of surface water management contributing to the reduction in pollutants that can be caused by flooding.

In this section we highlight some key aspects of what these new hybrid strategic intermediaries do in relation to infrastructure provision. Our aim here is to highlight the characteristics of strategic intermediary activity that involve reconfiguring relations within a production–consumption nexus.

Hybridity

'New intermediaries' are creating novel possibilities for sustainable practice. We use the words 'sustainable practice' deliberately to refer to the activities of both production and consumption as well as to both technological and social activities. New intermediaries point to sustainable practices that are hybrid relations of production and consumption, or technological and social. In relation to the technical versus the social solutions to sustainability, all the examples illustrate the role of the intermediaries in bringing together the social and the technical. The 'save-a-flush' campaign used a variety of promotional activities to motivate the application of a very simple technology. The housing association enabled the coupling of the application of water-saving devices for low-income households. And SWEL enabled a coupling between the technical solution of SuDS and the commercial interests of the company. Not only are the intermediaries hybrids, they also play a part in bringing together the social and the technical into new forms of social practice.

Selectivity

These 'new intermediaries' in their hybrid forms are in part characteristic of the transformation of utilities in general. The universal and standardized forms of provision characterized by the pre-1970s 'integrated modes' (Graham and Marvin, 2001) have been segmented into a range of forms of delivery as well as the differentiation of users into different groups of consumer. The new intermediaries are characteristic of this differentiation in their activities of drawing upon different and particular actors while in their effect targeting particular groups of users. Some water utility companies for example have targeted the 'save-a-flush' at higher-demand users. The housing associations have been concerned with the particular needs of low-income households, and SWEL is concerned to address the specific needs of business within the Lancashire area. Intermediation in all these cases involves processes of differentiating particular types of users who have particular demands or practices and addressing these through the particular reconfiguration of the production–consumption relationship. Even though in most cases the technology is indeed standardized, the role of the intermediaries is to enable their introduction into local contexts, selecting out particular social groups and sets of interests.

   The selectivity is therefore also transformative of infrastructural configurations. They involve creating new relationships between producers and users. The housing association renewed relationships between water companies, technology companies and tenants' associations. SWEL reconfigures the relationships between the regulator and commercial enterprises. The new intermediaries are creating new configurations between these various technical, organizational and network relations. This means selecting new boundaries, selecting particular actors, and selecting particular issues, logics and people when enabling the introduction of the new technologies.

Distributed

These dynamics also raise issues for understanding the location of sustainable practice. In selecting particular configurations of actors and relationships, new intermediaries also constitute a more localized and displaced form of sustainable practice. Save-a-flush devices become located in toilets in households, offices, schools and so on, and their success depends on distributed promotional activities across a range of media (from schools to TV), as well as their applicability within particular households and technological systems. In the case of SWEL, its expertise in being able to address the specific concerns of companies on site enables it to link the introduction of new technologies or practices to commercial interests. In the case of the housing association, its very specific relationship within Toxteth enabled the introduction of water-saving technologies. The success of intermediary activity lies precisely in the ability to introduce sustainable practices into local contexts, and through those local contexts bridging different social interests. Intermediary activity therefore becomes necessarily distributed and local, requiring specific contextual skills and expertise.

Valorization

The expertise of the intermediaries lies largely in their ability to generate new value from particular forms of relationships. In the case of save-a-flush, application in different contexts required different forms of valorization. Encouraging households to use the device would reduce overall water consumption, thus benefiting the water utilities, while for large organizations with metered water the device could save them money. The housing association was able to link the needs of low-income families with sustainable technologies and marketing issues of the water utility by implementing the concept of sustainable social housing. SWEL markets itself in terms of the commercial savings that companies can make by paying attention to sustainable management issues. So in different contexts, through particular forms of intermediation, value is generated for the utility companies, for regulators, for consumers and indeed for the intermediaries themselves in the process of reconfiguring the infrastructural relations.

SUSTAINABILITY BY PROXY?

By bringing together the social and the technical, and consumption and production practices, we have argued that new intermediaries are beginning to generate new locations for sustainable production and consumption by proxy. Intermediaries are not necessarily always successful, nor do they embody a particular approach to sustainability. Indeed there are many kinds of intermediaries with many roles, for example networking, campaigning, promoting, marketing and information dissemination. The three examples highlight particular characteristics of intermediaries. Their significance lies in an ability to strategically work across different interests in order to create new contexts for embedding new technologies and social practices that may, subject to evaluation, have key implications for sustainability. Such processes involve generating different meanings of such technologies and practices in varieties of contexts. While the UK government's promotion of sustainable consumption focuses on changing behaviours, the new intermediaries create different possibilities. With save-a-flush in the toilet, whether you know it or not, a flush of the WC involves a sustainable practice. You need not be an intentional sustainable consumer. It may be in your office. But by undertaking your normal consumption practice, your normal routine, through the 'save-a-flush' intermediary you are enrolled into sustainable practice. Indeed the location of sustainability has been shifted away from you and located in a proxy that now acts as if you intended to save water.

While intermediaries act as proxies for producers and consumers, they also insert technologies into new circuits of production–consumption that become proxies in themselves, acting for both the consumer and the producer. They become embedded into various network relations and translate between the two, bringing them together in one moment, indeed folding the distinction. Moving into a housing association tenancy in Toxteth works in much the same way. The housing association has become responsible for introducing and maintaining the sustainability of the water in the houses. Taking a shower or bath, using the dishwasher or the toilet, all involve a sustainable practice by proxy.

To talk of sustainability by proxy does not mean simply locating sustainability in either production or in technological solutions *per se*. Nor does it mean locating sustainability in either consumption or other social practices. Rather, sustainability by proxy is achieved by generating bridges and creating new hybrid forms that are at the same time both social and technical, production and consumption. Note though, that the achievement of sustainability by proxy has not been straightforward. It is not about shifting responsibility from the consumer to the producer (or vice versa). Rather it is about the integration of these processes in very specific ways, in specific contexts, between specific groups and so on. It can involve uncertainties (whether or not people flush the toilet more often or undertake the required maintenance of water recycling technology), which render the complexities of the process of intermediation difficult to model let alone anticipate.

CONCLUSION: WORKING FROM THE MIDDLE

The emergence of new intermediaries and the constitution of distributed relationships between production and consumption involve making visible the hidden work of infrastructures (Star, 1999). The unbundling of infrastructures has itself been a process of revealing the different aspects of production and consumption. However, whether it is the differentiation of the previously homogeneous consumer, the emphasis on the role of flushing the toilet or the possibilities of second-class water in the garden, the role of the intermediary has been to make visible, and condition, new possibilities for circuits of production–consumption which have implications for how we think about the location of sustainability. While traditional intermediaries, such as consultants and public health specialists, had a role within the traditional logics of infrastructure in which supply was to meet demand with minimal interruption, the emergence of new intermediary space involves the local configuration of multiple logics.

Where then, we might ask, do the solutions to sustainability lie? One approach is to develop particular policy initiatives or technological solutions and then to implement them. The problem of such 'top-down' approaches is the compromise that the context of implementation inevitably demands externalities as well as failures. An alternative approach is the focus on the consumer. Much attention has been devoted to raising awareness of water consumption, whether through promotional activities or financial disciplinary practices (that is metering). This we might talk of as a more 'bottom-up' approach to sustainability. Tensions between bottom-up and top-down approaches will always exist. This is the case whether discussing the solutions (politics) to issues of sustainability or trying to understand the emergence of sustainable social practices and technological innovations.

Focusing either on bottom-up (demand) or top-down (supply) for understanding the emergence of new intermediaries would be misleading. The emergence of the new intermediaries requires an understanding of their relational surfacing. This means understanding how, in relation to specific actors, logics, populations, practices and so on, they constitute new contexts enabling (making visible) possibilities that would not otherwise have been present. In other words the ways in which debates about sustainable consumption have focused on issues of production (for example more effective ways of recycling wastewater) or on consumption (for example shifting consumption practices towards using less water) can be understood in terms of tensions between top-down (production and supply) and bottom-up (consumption and demand). The emergence of new intermediaries involves a move beyond this divide to appreciate the co-constitution of production and consumption together, not as separate activities but as entwined in new circuits of production and consumption.

The question this chapter then raises is what are the implications of new intermediaries, emerging within the context of changing infrastructures, for understanding sustainable consumption? First, understanding infrastructural transition needs to take account of the emergence of new intermediaries that act in between the traditional divides between the consumer and the producer. These emerging actors generate novel and interesting ways of developing spaces for sustainable practice and we need to better understand the durability of these arrangements. Second, to distinguish consumption and production as separate spheres can be misleading. These new intermediaries suggest we need to work towards the ways in which sustainable practice combines moments of production and consumption to generate new circuits of sustainability. Third, the rise of new intermediaries means thinking beyond the capacity of the state, public agencies, social movements and commercial companies to explore how it is that the interrelationships between them, within particular contexts, can generate the possibilities for generating added value when contributing to sustainable practice. Finally, by recognizing the role being played by new intermediaries, it becomes necessary to explore the extent to which particular notions of social actors and of sustainability are being configured in ways that may reinforce problematic assumptions about the nature of social action and technological fixes.

The reconfigurations that new intermediaries generate increase the complexity of our understanding of the relationship between sustainable practices and social structures. Indeed the novelty that the new intermediaries bring is in reshaping relationships in new ways, creating new forms of opportunity and constraint, and generating new dynamics across different social groups and activities.

NOTES

1. See www.defra.gov.uk/news/2003/030206.htm
2. This chapter is derived from work undertaken by Will Medd and Simon Marvin as part of the EU F5 Intermediaries Project (EVK1-CT-2002-00115) which examines the rise of new intermediaries in the water sector. See www.irs-net.de/intermediaries.
3. See www.save-a-flush.co.uk.
4. See www.sustainable-development.gov.uk/uk_strategy/factsheetsaydyb/.
5. See www.sustainablehomes.co.uk/case_studies/cds.htm.

PART III

Infrastructural change and inflexibility

7. Institutional restructuring, entrenched infrastructures and the dilemma of overcapacity

Timothy Moss

INTRODUCTION

Opinion is divided over the impact of the liberalization and privatization of utility services on the consumption of energy and water resources. Proponents of liberalization argue that removing territorial monopolies and opening up utility markets to competition create powerful incentives for the efficient use of natural resources. Critics warn of a shift in priorities of commercialized utility companies towards maximizing profits and cutting costs at the expense of measures to protect the environment. This debate is conducted from the perspective of unacceptably high levels of energy and water consumption. The issue at stake is whether liberalized or state-protected markets offer the best chance of restraining demand and minimizing resource use.

While the assumption of high and growing levels of consumption underpinning this debate remains widely applicable there are growing instances across Europe where consumption is stagnating or even declining. Utility managers accustomed to expanding their physical networks to meet ever-growing demand for energy and water are, in some areas, having to confront an unfamiliar and unwelcome phenomenon: overcapacity in parts, or even all, of their infrastructure networks. This can be observed particularly in territories undergoing severe socio-economic structural change. The collapse or departure of major industrial consumers can sharply reduce consumption of energy and water in a particular area, as can depopulation or even suburbanization processes on a major scale. Dramatic examples of infrastructural overcapacity resulting from negative growth can be found across Eastern Germany (Koziol, 2002) and in parts of Central and Eastern Europe. Less extreme cases exist in certain rural areas and within towns and cities in Western Europe. Overcapacity in technical networks can also arise from existing plants losing their commercial viability in an increasingly competitive market of provision. The closure of less efficient power stations in liberalized energy markets such as the UK is a response to the under-utilization of existing electricity generation infrastructure.

How utilities in a liberalized market or under private ownership are responding to the novel challenge of overcapacity has not yet been addressed by research. This chapter presents an introduction to the issues involved, setting them in the context of recent research into the institutional restructuring of infrastructure systems and illustrating them with an empirical study of recent experiences of Berlin's water, power and gas utilities.[1] It draws on a growing body of knowledge on the reconfiguration of urban technical networks in the wake of broad trends towards the liberalization, privatization and commercialization of utility services (Graham, 2000a, 2000b; Graham and Marvin, 1996; Guy et al., 1996, 1997, 2001; Marvin and Guy, 1997; Offner, 2000). This literature has demonstrated how today's utility companies, under pressure to raise efficiency and compete for customers, are questioning the value of offering a standard, basic range of services to all customers at a fixed price and are consequently varying their services and prices to attract or retain customers and raise income (Graham, 2000a; Guy et al., 1997).

As several commentators have demonstrated convincingly, there is a distinct spatial dimension to these processes of differentiation (Graham, 2000a, 2000b; Guy et al., 1997; Marvin and Guy, 1997; Offner, 2000). Following the removal of territorial monopolies, utility companies are inclined to view and treat the area they serve no longer as a homogeneous space bounded by the limits of their physical network but as a web of spatially diverse sub-units often linked to wider national or even supranational grids. Working on this premise we might expect utility companies operating in liberalized markets to show increased concern for sections of their technical networks which are under utilized and, consequently, for territories they serve which are experiencing declining levels of resource consumption. In the past, under territorial monopoly conditions, the costs of under utilizing existing infrastructures could have been spread across all consumers; in liberalized utility markets this option is not commercially feasible. The problem of overcapacity today demands a solution. What kinds of solutions are being considered and pursued is explored here with a case study of Berlin.

The city of Berlin lends itself well to a study of overcapacity. Berlin has experienced rapid and severe de-industrialization following the reunification of Germany, and Berlin, in 1990. As industrial production has collapsed so has the consumption of water and energy by industrial users in particular. Utility companies, having anticipated further network expansion in the new German capital, are today having to come to terms with a declining or at best stagnating market punctuated with pockets of high and low demand. At the same time the institutional context of infrastructure provision in Berlin has changed markedly. The three principal utility companies for electricity, gas, and water and sewerage services were until recently owned by the city-state government. All three have been fully or partially privatized since 1997. Compared with other utilities in Germany they display a high degree of commercialization, particularly in the electricity and gas sectors, following the recent liberalization of the energy market in Germany. A case study of Berlin is therefore well suited to investigate problems of overcapacity experienced by an increasing number of utilities across Europe, from the perspective of a relatively advanced state of institutional reconfiguration.

This then is a study of the relationship between different dimensions of infrastructure systems – the material (transported natural resources), the technical (physical networks) and the social (organizations and institutions) – under conditions of declining resource consumption and growing market competition. In several respects the chapter offers unusual, but complementary, perspectives on the issues raised in this book:

- A different angle on consumption and consumers, particularly declining or stagnating consumption and its implications for technical infrastructures. It is not a study of consumers and how their use of resources is framed by choice, lifestyle constraints or daily routines, but an exploration of the absence of consumers or consumption in certain territories.
- A different angle on sustainable consumption. The chapter takes issue with the widely held assumption that reducing consumption is *per se* sustainable. It is argued that where reductions in resource use create major problems of under utilized infrastructure, the sustainable use of a natural resource can reduce the sustainability of an infrastructure network.
- A different angle on changing infrastructures of provision. Central to the chapter is the lack of adaptability of physical infrastructures to declining levels of consumption. Their physical and spatial embeddedness creates problems for utilities operating within a liberalized institutional framework.
- A different angle on the role of utility companies. The utility companies are not the agenda-setters familiar from the literature, providing new services and forging new relationships with their customers. Rather they are the victims of forces of socio-economic and institutional change largely beyond their control.

The chapter begins by examining what problems stagnating consumption is creating for entrenched infrastructures, in general and in Berlin. The following section analyses the recent institutional restructuring of Berlin's utilities against the backdrop of research into the reconfiguration of infrastructure systems. The final section draws on these findings to demonstrate how Berlin's utilities are responding to the challenge of overcapacity in parts of their technical networks. The conclusions reflect on how the empirical findings contribute to the body of knowledge on the reconfiguration of infrastructures of provision.

ENTRENCHED INFRASTRUCTURES AND DECLINING CONSUMPTION

Environmental Goods and Network Goods

Technical infrastructures play a central role in the consumption of natural resources. They determine the scale, timing and quality of water and energy flows at different stages of flow management, from the extraction of raw materials, via treatment of these resources (water purification, electricity generation) and their distribution to the collection, treatment and disposal of waste products from their consumption. Selected figures from Germany give an impression of the scale and importance of these resource flows. Some 32 per cent of Germany's entire energy consumption in 1999 (4705 PJ) was in the form of electricity distributed via the power stations and cables of power utilities (Statistisches Bundesamt, 2001, p. 230). The amount of wastewater treated in German sewage treatment plants each year is around 9.6 billion m^3, corresponding to one-fifth of the volume of Lake Constance (ATV-DVWK press statement of 22 February 2002). Besides the resource flows from provider to consumer, the processes of treatment and distribution themselves require a high energy and material input.

There exists a fundamental conflict of interest between the efficient use of natural resources on the one hand and of technical infrastructures on the other. The natural resources which technical infrastructures supply are environmental goods. To use these environmental goods efficiently means requiring fewer natural resources to satisfy the same, or greater, needs. The emphasis is on seeking ways of increasing resource productivity, as illustrated by the Factor Four concept (Von Weizsäcker et al., 1998). The artefacts by which these resources are supplied, the technical infrastructures themselves, are so-called network goods. The efficient use of network goods requires, by contrast, that they are used up to, or near, full capacity (Kaul et al., 1999, p. 5). The more a network good is used the more efficiently it operates, to the benefit of the operator and (theoretically at least) the end-consumer. In the case of infrastructure networks with their high fixed costs, the more energy and water are consumed the lower the unit costs of provision, so long as no infrastructure extension is required. Optimal management of technical networks requires maximizing the use of existing infrastructures up to a full capacity minus a safety reserve. The basic dilemma is therefore that maximizing the consumption of a network good is in the public interest while maximizing the consumption of an environmental good is not.

This dilemma is starkly revealed where consumption of the environmental good falls. Declining consumption levels pose a serious problem for infrastructure managers. Pipelines, cables and plants built to provide a certain quantity of energy or water according to expectations of peak demand operate less efficiently, and in some cases less effectively, if consumption remains significantly and continuously below full capacity (Koziol, 2002). The disappearance of a large industrial consumer may well have a positive effect on resource consumption on that particular site but it creates serious inefficiencies for the technical networks serving the site. A sudden and substantial drop in consumption levels does not reduce overall costs of running the networks significantly, since the proportion of fixed costs is very high. As a result higher unit charges are generally required to cover the investment costs. Even if older parts of the physical infrastructure have long since been written off financially, their continued use at near-maximum capacity is important for the economic performance of the network as a whole.

The crux of the problem lies in the entrenched nature of technical infrastructures. As the literature on large technical systems (LTS) has shown, there are physical and technical as well as social and institutional dimensions to the durability of technical infrastructures (Hughes, 1987; Summerton, 1994; Gökalp, 1992; Melosi, 2000). The physical artefacts, pipes, cables and plants are in a literal sense embedded in places. They are connected to other physical infrastructures, such as buildings, which are similarly territorially bound. The dominant techniques used to generate electricity or treat wastewater have often contributed to the spatial embeddedness of technical infrastructures, generating large-scale systems of supply or collection operating around the centralized node of a power station or sewage treatment plant. The resource flows themselves influence the degree of embeddedness of an infrastructure system according to their physical properties: water infrastructure is for this reason more spatially bound than electricity infrastructure. Beyond these physical-technical artefacts, social and institutional factors have also contributed substantially to the strong path-dependency of LTS such as infrastructure networks. Organizations, regulations and cultural values have always played a key role in shaping the development of infrastructure systems. As the LTS literature emphasizes, the 'system builders' and the institutional arrangements regulating infrastructure systems have, since the late nineteenth century, sought to consolidate, reinforce and develop further these technological systems (Hughes, 1987; Guy et al., 1997). The dominant logic of infrastructure managers in the past has been to build up and extend their technical networks to meet ever-growing demand. Against this backdrop of socio-technical drivers of infrastructure management it is clear why a decline in consumption levels poses such a fundamental challenge. Overcapacity not only threatens the economic efficiency and physical functionality of technical networks, it also undermines the traditional practices and underlying logics of infrastructure management.

Consumption Curves and Overcapacity in Post-unification Berlin

The problem of overcapacity and underefficiency in Berlin's technical networks emerged in the mid-1990s out of a combination of a legacy of network expansionism in the past and declining or stagnating localized demand following socio-economic restructuring. Since the building of the Berlin Wall in 1961 infrastructure managers on both sides of the divide had sought to maximize network capacity, for reasons of political security as well as to meet growing demand. Following unification in 1990 early predictions of rapid urban development and the decision for the federal government to locate in Berlin put pressure on the infrastructure managers to expand and upgrade the existing technical networks to meet the anticipated growth in demand. However, following the removal of state subsidies, subsidized prices and other protective measures which had long shielded the economies in both halves of the city from external competition, Berlin has experienced rapid and severe structural change characterized by de-industrialization, rising unemployment, a declining population and growing social polarization (Krätke and Borst, 2000). The city lost nearly one-half of its industrial workforce (47.5 per cent) between 1991 and 2000 and its population, counter to expectations, actually fell by 2.7 per cent between 1993 and 2000 (Statistisches Landesamt Berlin, 2001, pp. 33, 289).

This ongoing process of structural change has been one key factor behind the decline or stagnation of demand for the resources provided by utility companies. Other factors include the introduction of full-cost pricing in Eastern Berlin following unification, price increases to cover investment costs, the installation of water-saving technologies and, to a lesser extent, out-migration. The combined effect of these forces was to reduce water consumption in the city by 38 per cent between 1989 and 1999, and electricity consumption by 3 per cent between 1990 and 1999 (Statistisches Landesamt Berlin, 1994, 1999). Worst affected are those parts of the technical networks where industrial production has ceased. Some 1500 hectares of former industrial and commercial sites are no longer in use, representing 40 per cent of the city's total designated area for industrial production (SenSUT, 1997, p. 32). This is reflected in the figures for water and energy consumption. Between 1989 and 1999 water consumption by industrial and commercial customers declined by a massive 59 per cent. The Berlin water utility Berliner Wasserbetriebe has, in its own words, 'been badly hit by the downturn in industrial production' (Interview 3);[2] 'the loss of large customers has been particularly painful for us' (Interview 4). The power utility Bewag has also suffered the effects of de-industrialization, with consumption by the industrial sector in 1999 down by 35 per cent against 1990 levels (SenSUT, 1998a, p. 29). Today's brownfield sites have left gaping holes in the consumption patterns around which Berlin's technical networks were built.

As a result, all of Berlin's major utilities are now facing overcapacity in their networks, albeit to varying degrees and in particular subsections. Even the electricity networks, less spatially bound than water or gas, are affected:

> We have sites where industry has disappeared where huge cables are lying underused. A major customer could come in and get connected up within four weeks. (Interview 1)

> Parts of the district heating network suffer from over-capacity where significant numbers of previous users have switched to other heating forms, notably gas. Underutilised parts of the gas network pose a problem of sub-optimal operation for the gas utility. (Interview 2)

Worst affected are the water supply and wastewater disposal networks because of the greater decline in consumption and the greater spatial dependency of the physical infrastructure (Koziol, 2002, pp. 45–6). In Eastern Berlin the situation is particularly serious where 'over capacity exists in virtually all sections of the water supply network' (Interview 4). Beyond the economic problems of suboptimal performance, the underutilized parts of the water and sewerage networks are posing serious technical, environmental and public health problems. In areas where water consumption has fallen sharply, in particular the former industrial zones in Eastern Berlin, water is flowing so slowly through the supply pipes that it is reacting with the deposits that line them to the detriment of water quality and taste (Interview 4). As a countermeasure the water utility is currently flushing several hundred thousands of cubic metres of water a year through the affected pipes simply to maintain the required drinking water quality standards. This practice, referred to as 'artificial consumption' (Interview 4), is also used in the sewer system to prevent unpleasant smells caused by an inadequate flow of wastewater passing through certain underutilized sections of the sewer network. Falling water consumption has also caused groundwater levels in the city to rise. This development, though welcome in principle, is causing problems in areas of the city where rising groundwater is flooding cellars or otherwise impairing buildings. On certain brownfield sites the rising groundwater is coming into contact with contaminated soil, posing a serious threat to future drinking water resources from wells serving nearby waterworks (Lünser and Haeder, 1998, p. 69; Interview 4). In all these cases solutions to the problems are complicated by the absence of any end-user or consumer who could be called upon to pay for remedial measures.

INSTITUTIONAL RESTRUCTURING OF INFRASTRUCTURE SYSTEMS

Spatial Dimensions to Reconfiguration

At the same time as the unexpected direction of shifts in consumption patterns the institutions of infrastructure management in the city have been undergoing dramatic change. Before turning to these changes in Berlin it is worth reflecting on the spatial dimensions to the reconfiguration of technical infrastructures as described in the literature (Graham, 2000a, 2000b; Guy et al., 1997; Marvin and Guy, 1997; Offner, 2000). Generally speaking, utility companies faced with the removal of territorial monopolies and increased competition are adopting novel spatial strategies. Rather than managing their service areas as a homogeneous whole protected from outside competition, they are looking beyond and within their traditional territories to reduce costs and where possible exploit new markets. We can observe three dimensions to the spatial reconfiguration of technical infrastructures subject to commercialization: territorial penetration, expansion and differentiation. Territorial penetration entails competing utilities providing goods and services to customers within a former territorial monopoly served by another utility company. Territorial expansion refers to the process of utility companies extending their area of provision by means of company takeovers, buying up concessions or forming territorial partnerships with neighbouring utilities. Territorial differentiation is the term for the distinction utility companies are increasingly making between areas of their networks which are performing well and those which are not. This phenomenon, the least familiar in the public debate, is worth outlining in more detail because it is particularly pertinent to the issue of declining resource use raised in this chapter.

Guy et al. have provided a simple model of 'hot spots' and 'cold spots' to illustrate how commercialized utility companies increasingly distinguish between different sections of their network (Guy et al., 1997). 'Hot spots' represent those areas where localized demand is high and in danger of exceeding existing capacities for provision. They are usually territories experiencing dynamic growth. These could be whole urban regions but are more likely to be those areas where lucrative customers are located, such as the gated communities and Business Improvement Districts studied by Graham (2000b). 'Cold spots' by contrast are areas of underutilized technical networks where demand is low or stagnating. Cold spots are often areas of decline which are, for the service provider, 'zones of limited commercial opportunity' (Guy et al., 1997). It is important to note that cold spots can exist not only in rural or peripheral areas but also in those sections of an otherwise prosperous conurbation affected by structural decline, such as brownfield sites. In the past their existence posed little problem: with a territorial monopoly utility companies could distribute costs among all customers. Under a liberalized utility market however these cold spots can become a commercial liability. The option for utility companies is either to neglect them, that is provide only the minimum service required by law or service contract, or to seek actively to raise demand by attracting new customers to locate in their cold spots.

Reconfiguration in Berlin

Berlin's principal utility companies for power, gas, and water and wastewater services are currently undergoing rapid and substantial transformation in response to privatization and liberalization processes. As across Germany, Berlin's utility companies have long histories of municipal ownership and management. Prior to 1997 the city-state still owned Berliner Wasserbetriebe and had a majority shareholding in Bewag and the gas utility GASAG. In order to help offset the city's major debt and budget crisis of the mid-1990s however, it was decided to sell off all or part of these companies, Bewag and Berliner Wasserbetriebe being very lucrative. Bewag was fully privatized in 1997, GASAG in 1998 and a 49.9 per cent stake in Berliner Wasserbetriebe was sold in 1999, bringing the city revenue of 3.76 billion euros in total.

The second major institutional change has been the liberalization of the energy market in Germany. This occurred concurrently with the privatization offensive in Berlin; the prospect of liberalization was indeed used as an argument in favour of privatizing the city's utilities. Since 1998 the generation and trading of electricity and since 2000 the trading of gas have been liberalized in Germany (Cronenberg, 1998; Monstadt, 2000; Schneider, 1999). The impact of liberalization in Berlin has been most notable in the intense competition for large commercial, industrial and public customers in the electricity sector, where Bewag has lost some important clients. The company's market share for electricity sales in Berlin had fallen to 86 per cent by the end of the financial year 2000/2001 with the sharpest decline among industrial customers (Bewag, 2001, p. 10). Inroads into GASAG's monopoly of gas supply have been as yet very limited. By contrast, water supply services in Germany remain the responsibility of local authorities and are protected by territorial monopolies. However, by nature of its legal status, Berliner Wasserbetriebe is entitled to provide services under contract to other authorities, enabling the company to expand its market into surrounding municipalities and abroad following unification. Moreover the issue of whether to liberalize or modernize water supply services in Germany is currently under discussion. For this reason Berliner Wasserbetriebe, as one of Germany's largest water utilities, is preparing to take advantage of potential market opportunities in the future.

The effect of both privatization and liberalization has been to radically alter the commercial strategies of the three utilities over a short space of time. In line with familiar trends in other industrialized countries the utilities are taking various steps to raise efficiency, increase their market share and develop new markets. Expenditure on staff and investments is being cut back sharply. Bewag reduced staff levels by 57 per cent between 1992 and 2001, GASAG by 41 per cent between 1995 and 1999 (Bewag, 1995, p. 47; Bewag, 2001, p. 22; GASAG, 1999, p. 25). In 1997 Berliner Wasserbetriebe cut back its ten-year investment plan radically from 21 to 12.2 billion DM (SenSUT, 1998b). The energy utilities in particular are seeking to win and retain customers by providing new services and cutting prices. Bewag and GASAG advertise a wide range of services 'beyond the meter', such as energy-saving audits, load management and the operation of block-type combined heat and power (CHP) plants. Electricity prices have been cut following liberalization, especially for larger customers (Bewag, 2000, pp. 10–11); gas prices for major commercial customers fell by 47 per cent between 1995 and 1998 (GASAG, 1999). In addition, all three utilities are drawing on their new international partners to improve internal management and gain access to new markets. Berliner Wasserbetriebe in particular is developing a multi-utility profile, for instance offering a single-charge package for electricity, telephone and Internet services via a subsidiary (Avida) and using its existing physical networks to house telecommunications cables.

Beyond these phenomena familiar from the literature on reconfiguration we can observe some important distinctions which indicate that the process of transformation is neither uniform across all utilities nor undisputed within them. Firstly, the city's three principal utilities are moving in a similar direction, but at different speeds and with different points of emphasis. The degree of liberalization is clearly important in determining how far a utility company seeks to cut costs and create new markets. However, the territorial embeddedness of the technical networks appears equally important in framing a utility's response to pressures for change. The degree to which an urban infrastructure network is integrated into external networks, the availability of the natural resource in question and the ease with which it can be transported have a significant bearing on the spatial strategies of utility companies in particular (on the scale effects of different infrastructure networks, see Graham, 2000a, p. 118). This helps explain the greater responsiveness of a water and wastewater utility than a power utility to the problem of cold spots. Secondly, tensions exist between competing logics of infrastructure management even within a single utility. This is evident between engineering units following the traditional supply logic and marketing units keen to create greater customer awareness. Recently hired marketing specialists complain about the 'persistent public sector mentality' (Interview 3) and 'disregard for individual customer's needs' (Interview 1) of some of their own colleagues in engineering departments. The engineers, often long-standing employees responsible for building up today's physical networks, continue to perceive their task as providing universal and secure basic services for all (Interview 4). It would appear from the evidence of the Berlin case that the process of reconfiguration is less clear-cut and more piecemeal than often portrayed in the literature.

COPING WITH OVERCAPACITY

Following the model of spatial differentiation between hot spots and cold spots of infrastructure networks we might expect Berlin's utility companies to be looking more closely than in the past at the performance of subsections of their networks. Although the shifts in commercial strategies are relatively new there are already clear signs of spatial differentiation being practised by the three utility companies, albeit to differing degrees. Infrastructure managers are indeed taking greater interest in consumption trends in different parts of the city and the effects these are having on network viability. They are displaying particular concern for cold spots: the underutilized parts of their networks.

With the following strategies of spatial differentiation the three utility companies are striving to combat problems of overcapacity.

Spatially Sensitive Data

The utilities are exploring new methods of gaining more detailed data on consumption patterns which are spatially and user specific. Berliner Wasserbetriebe is currently developing a data system which will enable it to identify water consumption profiles according to customer type, urban neighbourhood and subsection of its water supply network. This will help the company 'to plan for plant closures and the redirection of sewage flows' (Interview 3). GASAG is already building up a database on gas consumption which will enable the utility to determine more precisely the performance of individual sections of its supply network (Interview 2).

Commercially Viable Sub-units

GASAG intends to use the above data to improve the economic performance of each section of its gas supply network, and not simply the network as a whole. In future 'each sub-network [will be] responsible for its performance – it must be economically viable on its own' (Interview 2). Whereas in the past decisions to build new or expand existing gas pipelines were dependent primarily on the existence or anticipation of demand, in future the impact of these investments on the profitability of the relevant section of the network will be taken into account. For example when a large customer requires connecting to the gas network GASAG will calculate not only the specific costs of the investment but also how the consumption of the customer is likely to affect the performance and capacity of that network section.

Risk Minimization with Infrastructure Investments

Negative experiences with greenfield development sites in the past, where resource consumption fell well short of predictions, have prompted the utilities to adopt precautionary measures to minimize the financial risks involved in funding major infrastructure extensions. In the past the utilities were required by the state government of Berlin to provide for the necessary physical infrastructure up to the property boundary and would recoup the costs via service charges paid by all their customers. Under today's commercial climate they are less willing to take this risk. GASAG now obliges investors to enter into a contract which ensures compensation to the gas utility if the quantity of gas consumed following completion of the site development does not reach an agreed level (Interview 2). Berliner Wasserbetriebe has introduced contractual agreements whereby the developer undertakes to build the necessary infrastructure extensions which are subsequently operated by the water utility (Interviews 3 and 4).

Plant Closure

The utilities are closing down plants which are not commercially viable, especially in those areas where demand is falling sharply. Berliner Wasserbetriebe has for this reason already shut down four waterworks and one sewage treatment plant since unification. There are advanced plans to close a further sewage treatment plant at Falkenberg and two waterworks at Johannistal and Jungfernheide (Interview 4). Bewag was considering the closure of several of its CHP stations in the city until a federal law was introduced, on the initiative of the Berlin state government, to protect existing CHP plants from competition.

We can observe therefore that Berlin's three major utilities are keen to optimize use of their existing networks. They are showing a growing interest in how different subsections of their technical networks perform, distinguishing between hot spots and cold spots. They are taking steps to minimize the risk of future overcapacity and to reduce current overcapacity. The utility companies are even showing interest in directing urban development to areas where their existing networks are operating below capacity. In the words of a GASAG representative: 'We are very keen to keep new customers off greenfield sites and to locate them where possible in those parts of the network where we have free capacity' (Interview 2).

However, the utility companies are not actively involved in attracting investors to their infrastructure cold spots. This is because the infrastructure managers are sceptical of their ability to influence the decisions of either investors or the city's economic development and planning agencies. In their opinion infrastructure provision is not generally regarded as an important location factor: 'the influence of infrastructure on location decisions is relatively small' (Interview 1). There are also difficulties in matching investors' multiple infrastructure requirements to specific underutilized sites. Furthermore utility companies are usually involved very late in the decision-making process. As an engineer from Berliner Wasserbetriebe commented: 'Investors discover far too late how high infrastructure investment costs will be. By that time the decision where to locate has usually been made' (Interview 4). Above all they are pessimistic at the prospects of any new occupants of former industrial sites consuming past levels of energy and water and thereby solving the problem of underutilization: 'The problem for Berlin is whole industries have disappeared. And they won't come back. Whatever takes their place will of course be far less energy-intensive than the old production plants' (Interview 1).

CONCLUSIONS

The purpose of this chapter has been to shed fresh light on the debate over the current reconfiguration of technical infrastructures from the unusual perspective of declining or stagnating consumption. Whereas other studies have focused on efforts to curb unsustainable levels of demand for natural resources provided by utility companies, this chapter has demonstrated how underutilization and overcapacity in technical networks can render them unsustainable. Distinctive features of this narrative have been the unexpected downturn of demand curves, the lack of consumers and the role of utility companies as victims rather than initiators of change. The chapter has used a case study of Berlin as a window on these developments, chosen for its combined experience of socio-economic restructuring and utility reconfiguration in the 1990s. The case of Berlin in its particular configuration may be unique, but the issue of coping with declining, stagnating or at least unpredictable levels of resource use is very real for many infrastructure managers today, especially in areas hard hit by de-industrialization and out-migration in Central and Eastern Europe.

Looking at the causes of declining demand for energy and water this study has revealed in particularly stark form how dependent utilities can be on forces of urban development beyond their control. In the case of Berlin, processes of de-industrialization and socio-spatial restructuring have altered patterns of land use and resource consumption across the city, but particularly in certain areas. Declining or stagnant consumption levels now pose a major challenge to utility managers accustomed to extending their networks to meet ever-growing demand. They are seriously concerned at the emergence of underutilized cold spots diminishing the financial returns and jeopardizing the technical effectiveness of their networks. Initial responses to this problem, such as developing area-specific performance standards and minimizing investment risks on undeveloped sites, indicate heightened sensitivity for spatial structures and urban dynamics on the part of utility managers. The trend towards greater spatial differentiation documented in the literature would appear to apply therefore not solely to zones of high commercial opportunity but also to underutilized sections of a utility's networks.

The response of the utility companies to the challenge of overcapacity can be explained only in part by their commercialization following liberalization and privatization. The problem of underutilized networks has certainly become particularly serious in more competitive utility markets. The fundamental problem however has to do with the embeddedness of infrastructure systems and their inability to adapt adequately to consumption trends which buck the long-term pattern of continuous growth. This embeddedness is of a physical, institutional and socio-economic nature. We have observed, firstly, how the degree of spatial dependency of physical networks and the natural resources they transport influences a utility's interest in adopting spatially differentiated strategies of infrastructure management. Where spatial dependence is high, as in the case of Berlin's water utility, so is spatial differentiation; where it is low, as with the power utility, interest in the performance of subsections of a network is less marked. This suggests the need for a more sector-specific understanding of reconfiguration processes. The case study illustrates, secondly, the dependence of infrastructure systems on the territories they serve and in particular on the socio-economic development of these territories. The reconfiguration of infrastructure networks needs therefore to be understood in the context of the reconfiguration of urban space and land-use forms. Finally, the embeddedness of traditional logics of infrastructure management should not be underestimated. Liberalization and privatization do not transform utility companies overnight. The transformation process is characterized not simply by the replacement of one logic by another, but by the interaction of competing logics within a utility company. Appreciating this complex process of interaction would help explain why the reconfiguration of infrastructure networks can proceed along very different pathways and at different speeds.

Looking beyond the utility companies this study raises some important questions about how we conceive of sustainable consumption in contexts of socio-economic restructuring or decline. Achieving more sustainable forms of consumption is generally interpreted in terms of minimizing resource use, either by increasing resource productivity or altering consumption practices. This study, while not challenging the general thrust of this argument, has illustrated an important limitation to the pursuit of ever-lower levels of consumption and ever-higher rates of resource efficiency. The distribution of natural resources, such as water and energy, depends on physical infrastructures whose effective and efficient operation requires maximizing utilization up to a certain limit. If these infrastructures are used substantially below this limit serious inefficiencies are incurred, given the high level of fixed costs involved. The two common responses to inefficiencies of this kind are to raise unit prices, passing the financial losses on to the consumer, and to encourage greater consumption, at odds with environmental objectives of resource efficiency. In this sense the underutilization of technical infrastructures often proves unsustainable from a social and environmental, as well as an economic, perspective.

This chapter has shown how the distinction between environmental goods and network goods is useful for conceptualizing these divergent demands on infrastructure management. For researchers of sustainable consumption the challenge is therefore to identify and explain areas of resonance and dissonance between the logics of sustainable consumption and sustainable provision and illustrate how these might affect the transition to the more sustainable use of water and energy. The challenge for urban planners, utility managers, environmental regulators and others responsible for infrastructure systems is to seek ways of minimizing resource use which avoid excessive negative effects on the physical infrastructures. In particularly severe situations where such effects are unavoidable, a reduction of infrastructure capacity, where technically and economically feasible, is an option which can allow the relationship between provision and consumption to be reset at a new, lower level.

NOTES

1. Parts of this chapter appeared in *Environment and Planning A*, 2003, vol.35, no. 3, pp. 511–29 under the title 'Utilities, land-use change, and urban development: brownfield sites as "cold spots" of infrastructure networks in Berlin'.
2. Interviews with representatives from the Berlin power utility Bewag, business unit for commercial relations, 7 December 2000 (Interview 1); the Berlin gas utility GASAG, business unit for industrial and commercial customers, 4 July 2001 (Interview 2); the Berlin water and sewerage utility Berliner Wasserbetriebe, business unit for customer services, 10 July 2001 (Interview 3); the Berlin water and sewerage utility Berliner Wasserbetriebe, business unit for pipeline systems, 11 July 2001 (Interview 4).

8. Transport infrastructures: a social–spatial–temporal model

Noel Cass, Elizabeth Shove and John Urry[1]

INTRODUCTION

Changes to transport infrastructures, whether the construction of new networks or the reconfigured use of existing systems, have implications which reach beyond the management of mobility, narrowly defined. Building on the idea that patterns of mobility have to do with changing patterns of social life and urban development, this chapter has a number of ambitions. One is to articulate and further explore the social dimensions and determinants of travel, broadening the concept of transport infrastructures from a quantitative analysis of linear connections and timetables to focus especially on aspects of spatial and temporal coordination. We address this issue from various angles, thinking about the collective ordering of space and time, and about how individuals schedule and organize their own mobility within given infrastructures.

Another intention is to explore the importance of time(s) in infrastructures, time having different values for different individuals, and over which various actors have diverse amounts of control and power. We draw attention to a 'politics of time' in relation to transport and mobility, one related to individual and infrastructural flexibility and dependency.

Our third aim is to offer evidence of the difficulties that a conceptualization of transport infrastructures as social–spatial–temporal constellations raises for attempts to grasp their nature in empirical study. In trying to find a mid-level of analysis between the collective transport system and the individual's experience of it, and in attempting to pay heed to all the relevant aspects that combine to configure mobility and the infrastructures within which it takes place, we seem to have discovered an important uncertainty principle. We may be able to uncover where and when people are able to travel, or to theorize the reasons, both individual and social, that drive observable increases in mobility, but connecting one 'level' to the other presents intimidating layers of complexity.

This chapter draws on a study of transport-related social exclusion, an issue that has received increasing attention in the transport policy world. This policy concern indicates the significance of mobility for full membership of society, hence central government's interest in ensuring that transport demand management strategies and policies to reduce congestion do not disproportionately impact on those whose (lack of, or constrained) mobility is already implicated in their exclusion.

We start with an abstract model of social–spatial inclusion and exclusion, defining this as an emergent property of the interaction between social obligations, individual resources and physical infrastructures, as illustrated in Figure 8.1.

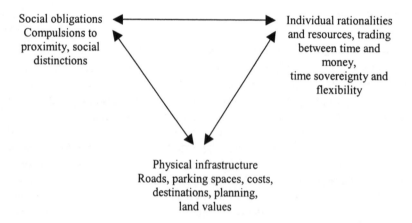

Figure 8.1 Social–spatial inclusion and exclusion as an emergent property of the interaction between social obligations, individual resources and physical infrastructures

This figure points out the tensions between the individual and the collective levels within the framework of physical infrastructure, and it also draws attention to social and temporal aspects often omitted in analyses of transport and mobility. With this model in mind, we show that an understanding of transport infrastructures must not simply describe networks of connectivity but take into account the social and individual motivations, resources and capabilities that together constitute the 'infrastructure in action'. Before trying to develop this model so as to capture and describe infrastructures of mobility and associated patterns of social–spatial inclusion and exclusion, we comment on general trends in transport and travel and on their social, temporal and spatial determinants. We build on these observations in proposing a different way of analysing transport infrastructures. In conclusion we comment on the challenges this represents for social science and for policy.

TRANSPORT AND TRAVEL

Travel Growth and Policies

Exceptional increases in car driving and the growth of suburban living have extended patterns of daily personal travel in all European countries, especially since the end of the Second World War. British citizens currently make around 1000 domestic journeys a year, spending about 360 hours per year travelling (DTLR, 2001, Table 2.1, Table 3.1). The increase in total distance travelled over the past half-century, from about 0.5 billion passenger-kilometres in the 1950s to about 7.5 billion passenger-kilometres in 2000, is staggering. Even since 1990 there has been a 42 per cent increase in distance travelled per person (SEU, 2002). Personal travel is expected to double again by 2025 (Doyle and Nathan, 2001, pp. 3–4; Urry, 2003a) accompanied by a dramatic reduction in walking.

These trends in (especially automobile) mobility cause significant problems for transport infrastructures. Firstly, there is the long-term infrastructural immobility of existing motorways, junctions, slip roads, underpasses, bridges and tunnels. These infrastructures are based on the average size of cars and lorries, which are built for at least four people despite 70 per cent of journeys in the USA involve driving alone (Putnam, 2000) and historically derive from the shape of the horse-drawn carriage. At the same time as mobility increases, the amount of infrastructure per car is declining and this makes driving increasingly demanding everywhere. Secondly, environmental concerns have made inroads into transport policy, with transport identified as the fastest-growing sector contributing to the emission of greenhouse gases. Growth in this sector outweighs cuts elsewhere, making progress towards local, national and global goals such as the Kyoto commitments increasingly fraught (see the well-known critiques in Whitelegg, 1997; Adams, 1999).

Although they take different forms, infrastructural stresses are nothing new. It is therefore instructive to take stock of policy responses. We identify three, outlined below.

'Predict and provide' models suppose that increased mobility is a desirable good. Predictions of future car use, based on extrapolations from the present, have been used to legitimize and justify the development of new road schemes explicitly designed to meet anticipated demand. Such an approach governed transport planning up to the mid-1990s (in the 1986 Department of

Transport (DfT), there were 12 500 civil servants concerned with roads, 72 working on rail and 53 working on public transport; Vigar, 2002, p. 58). These models arguably produced 'successful' increases in car-based mobility (see the critique in Whitelegg, 1997; Adams, 1999; Vigar, 2002), as shown by the extraordinary growth of car movement within the second half of the twentieth century, as opposed to mobility using other modes of travel. By the mid-1990s car travel was a dozen or so times greater, swamping all other modes of mobility (see Vigar, 2002, p. 12; Axhausen, 2002). In effect policies of this kind seek to conquer space and manage flow and thus time by increasing capacity for automobility.

Second, there is the more recent policy of the 'new realism' dating from the early 1990s. This recognizes that the expansion of the road network has the very effect of increasing the amount of car-based travel (although many predictions were not in fact fully met: see Vigar, 2002, p. 49). Under 'new realism', the focus shifts from road engineering and its policy network linked into local authorities, the construction industry and the DfT, to more difficult forms of social engineering, involving various forms of demand management. The 'new realism' requires many organizations to develop plans and policies, at local and national or European levels. It implies (amongst other things) improved public transport, better facilities for cyclists and pedestrians, advanced traffic management, more effective use of land-use planning and a much broader analysis of how transport impacts upon many aspects of the environment (see Vigar, 2002, pp. 15, 46, 58, 67). This model focuses quite explicitly on managing and changing the relation between space and time (in different ways for different sectors of the population) for economic and/or environmental reasons (see DETR, 1998b).

Third, there are plans and processes that result in increased 'commercial segmentation' and the development of a splintered urbanism (see Graham and Marvin, 2001, pp. 249–52 on 'automotive secession'). In this analysis the actions of very many different private corporations and public authorities effectively shatter the urban form, resulting in an increased segmentation of markets and products. Automobility has always effected certain separations, of work from suburban home from leisure spaces from shops and so on. Social exclusion is very significantly spatialized through the increasing dominance of the car, taken to the furthest extreme with the gated cities of North America (Graham and Marvin, 2001). This exclusionary logic is embedded in plans for electronic road pricing (ERP), road-user charging or the workplace parking levy. In due course, and in the cause of 'ecological modernization', road networks may become computerized systems supporting new practices of privatized commodification, control and exclusion.

Transport and travel cannot be separated from the evolving character of urban form and life, the policies and practices of given local authorities and national bodies, and the changing technologies and products developing within the corporate sector. More importantly, consideration of transport infrastructures cannot be divorced from an analysis of some of the 'social' processes that determine travel flows and structure the social–technical–temporal properties of transport systems as a whole.

Social Dimensions

In thinking about the social determinants of travel we start by observing that it is often not necessary for people to travel physically since there are many other forms of communication between them. These include the letter, telegram, telephone, e-mail, videoconference, text messaging, radio, television and so on. A variety of alternatives to physical travel are available. The key notion in explaining why travel is on occasions necessary is the 'compulsion to proximity': people travel in order to be co-present with others for certain periods of time (see Urry, 2002, 2003b). Travel is embodied and as a result people are physically co-present with workmates, business colleagues, friends, partner or family; they bodily encounter some particular landscape or townscape, or are physically present at a particular live event. In other words travel results in intermittent moments or intermittent periods of physical proximity to particular peoples, places or events. This proximity is felt to be obligatory, appropriate or desirable. It is not a matter of choice on that occasion.

In relationship to other people, 'thick' co-presence involves rich, multi-layered and dense face-to-face conversation (see Boden and Molotch, 1994; Urry, 2002) in which misunderstandings can be corrected, and commitment and sincerity can be directly assessed. Especially important is how this enables the building up of trust, something that gets worked at and involves a joint performance by those party to such co-present conversations. Of course physical co-presence can also reveal the lack of trust, demonstrating that somebody is not to be believed or that the deal should not be done. 'Official' meetings are often multifunctional, being good for making decisions, seeing how one is heard, executing standard procedures and duties, distributing rewards, status and blame, reinforcing friendship as well as distance, judging commitment, having an enjoyable time and so on. They are the social 'glue' that binds organizations together, with managers in the US spending up to half of their time in face-to-face meetings and more working with and evaluating colleagues through extensive physical co-presence (Boden and Molotch, 1994, p. 272). This reflects an apparent shift from an individual work ethic to a collective team ethic in which face-to-face social and leadership skills are especially valued within organizations.

The extent to which social networks underpin mobility patterns is greater than much research assumes. The degree of perceived 'compulsion' is underlined by the Rowntree Study that reveals 'almost 7.5 million people [in the UK] are too poor to engage in social activities considered necessary like visiting friends and family, attending weddings and funerals or having celebrations on special occasions' (Gordon et al., 2000). By implication, mobility is required to satisfy social needs and to meet those social obligations intrinsic to the 'good life'.

Social processes affecting the nature of such demands include changing household composition, there now being many more, smaller household units and therefore greater need to travel between dispersed members. There are increasingly global migration patterns with families strung out across the world (Cohen, 1997). Leisure time is being restructured around more, shorter visits rather than the standard two-week holiday. Computer-mediated communications are deconstructing organizations that were once huge centres of work and enforced proximity, and organizational relations with consumers are increasingly virtual or remote. These trends no longer demand the physical unity and organizational hierarchy of very large numbers of workers working within a single 'co-present' site with resulting works trains or buses (Evans and Wurstler, 2000, pp. 107–9). All these processes modify the possibilities of, and need for, intermittent co-presence that travel can afford, and therefore play havoc with some modernist notions of coordinated travel and transport infrastructures.

There are also complex connections between the flows of people and the transporting of goods. Changes in the urban infrastructure involve changes in the transport of goods, to shops, households, factories, offices, wholesalers and so on. But where goods go, people may also go, as with out-of-town shopping centres. Alternatively people and goods may travel in different patterns, as when goods are delivered to the doorstep following a telephone or Internet order. Some developments of e-commerce reduce visits to shopping centres and increase the delivery of individual items, and it is uncertain whether these developments will reduce mobility.

Finally, deliberate interventions in the form of urban and suburban planning continue to shape the density of the built environment and the distances travelled by both people and things. To complicate matters further, relevant developments, including the long-term dislocations of home, work, school, shopping and leisure, lie beyond the control of any single 'actor'. In effect, the distribution of options foreclosed and still open (that is the extent and direction of path-dependency and future flexibility) results from a combination of processes, including:

- The rise of megabusiness (such as supermarket chains) which increasingly wipe out other options and lock people into less sustainable travel patterns.
- The hegemony of ideologies of choice and competition in many areas of life. For example ranking schools by exam league tables engenders social competition, portrayed as choice, and ruptures the link between home, neighbourhood and school.
- The increasing perception that certain social groups are especially vulnerable – children, older people, ethnic minorities, women – and these need to be made 'safer' in their mobility.
- Localized effects of globalization in work situations, such as flexibilizing work, dual-income households, short-term contracts and job insecurity, the rise of edge-of-town employment zones, all of which extend travel-to-work patterns.
- Developments in previously local leisure and health facilities that are now often 'peripherally centralized' in edge-of-town centres.

Such changes evidently impact on the physical configuration of transport infrastructures. However, the engines driving such changes are largely social in nature, having to do with new uses of time and space associated with changing relationships between home, work, leisure and consumption. Having drawn attention to the social configuration of mobility, we now show the implications for the temporal dimensions of travel and transport.

Temporal Dimensions

How household members manage their various compulsions to proximity relates to the individual and collective juggling of key resources, including those of time and money. Juggling techniques involve quite complex assessments of the temporal advantages and drawbacks of different transport modes and infrastructures, involving for example knowledge of likely delays, possible delays, periodicities of availability and reliability (Cass et al., 2003, Chapter 4). Strategies depend on the resources and ambitions that people bring to such situations, some having more time than money or vice versa. The paradigmatic examples here are of a professional with plenty of money but a very tight timetable, compared with someone who is unemployed who 'possesses' almost limitless time but few financial resources.

The very idea of 'trading' between time and money, for instance paying more for a faster train, to use a particular road or to avoid waiting, implies a common currency of temporal value, exemplified by the phrase 'time is money'. Although a common formulation, this equation obscures two dimensions both relevant to an understanding of social division and the structuring of space and time (see Adams, 1999).

First, time is not valued in the abstract, but in terms of how it might be put to use. For example it might be assumed that the unemployed are 'rich in time', but as many writers about time have pointed out, being rich in time involves having time to perform meaningful tasks (Reisch, 2001). For many who have 'time to spare', such tasks are absent, leading to frustration and boredom.

Second, and depending on the route and distance involved, certain modes of transport (hitchhiking, walking and to a lesser extent cycling) are only possible for those with 'time to spare'. In opting for these modes rather than faster alternatives, there is a conscious trade-off between time and the quality of the experience. As Cass (2002) reflects:

> Hitching onto campus when I have the bus fare, in my case, is a conscious tactic of trading resources. I keep my money in my pocket, risk a long wait for a lift, but trade the speed and comfort of a car and the sociability of talking with the driver for the slowness, over-crowding and anti-sociability of public transport.

A further point to notice is that the relation between time and mobility is not fixed. Put simply, congestion convinces some people to leave their car at home but as road space is opened up by the diversion of journeys or their displacement on to other modes, others take advantage of this new freedom and instantly negate it. Other positive feedback loops relate to the demand for temporal coordination. If more commuters seek to arrive by 9 am it becomes necessary for each to start out earlier to anticipate congestion and still arrive 'on time'. Rush hours are therefore extended as a result (Cass et al., 2003).

The varying valuations of time outlined above have a bearing on how people organize their daily lives. The morning rush hour is for instance a consequence of multiple individuals each striving to reach appointed locations of co-presence (schools, workplaces and so on) at an appointed time so as to permit synchronized proximity. The modernist institutionalization of the 'normal' working day has historically structured both time and space and the transport infrastructures necessary to organize such synchronization (Adam, 1990, 1995, 1998; Zerubavel, 1979).

While collective scheduling continues to be an important coordinating force, social–temporal patterns are changing. The '24-hour society' creates opportunities for distributions of activity not possible under other more rigidly scheduled regimes. One consequence of an apparent breakdown of what used to be predictably scheduled events (like mealtimes, times for social interaction and times for work) is that people are increasingly obliged to negotiate the details of co-presence case by case and via the mobile phone actually 'on the move'. For some at least, the scheduling of social life appears to be an increasingly 'do-it-yourself' operation – a question of arranging encounters around flexitimes, and of searching for common slots between people with idiosyncratic schedules (see Hulme and Peters, 2001). In such contexts, controlling the schedules of others, of when and where to meet, constitutes an increasingly important asset of power in a politics of time.

While some people may have greater temporal flexibility than before, the consequent need to organize ever more complex diaries (more complex because other peoples' time is also more fragmented and less formally controlled), generates distinctive pressures for coordination and what we might call 're-coordination' in time and space (as Laurier and Philo, 2001, describe in the case of mobile workers). Southerton (2003) argues that in coping with these pressures people cram multiple events and activities together, creating an intense busyness so as to carve out periods of 'quality time' elsewhere in their schedule. Though developed person by person, such strategies have cumulative consequences for the density and distribution of transport 'hot' and 'cold' spots of space and time across the complex social world.

In this context flexibility is potentially as valuable as the amount of time itself. In short, patterns of mobility are not only geared around the reduction of time (in the 'time is money' sense), but also around the management of timing. This emphasis is evident in the spread of many 'just-in-time' familial machines. Devices like the telephone, radio, household TV and VCR, the PC, heating appliances, the camera or camcorder, and especially the family car are mainly stored within the home or garage. Easily operated and always accessible, they come to life when the family requires them and not when experts or the state determines. Their use depends upon personalized or familial time and not upon the objective, public timetable of the railway or airline (see Urry, 2000, pp. 191–2; Silverstone, 1993). Being one amongst this family of 'time-machines', cars extend where people can go to and hence shape what they are able to do.

Much of what many people now think of as 'social life' could not be undertaken without the temporal flexibilities of the car and its availability 24 hours a day. It is possible to leave late by car, to miss connections, to travel in a relatively timeless fashion. Not only that, some people derive pleasure from simple flexibility, in travelling when they want to, along routes that they choose, finding new places unexpectedly, stopping for relatively open-ended periods of time, and moving on when they desire (Sheller and Urry, 2000). Stradling (2002, p. 4) summarizes much survey evidence that brings out the importance for many people of the 'freedom to go where I want when I want'. Cars are what Shove (1998) terms a 'convenience device' of contemporary society, a device that makes complex, harried 'just-in-time' patterns of social life possible, but only for those families owning or with access to cars through renting, hiring taxis, or getting lifts from friends or family. By contrast, research reveals the time-inflexibility for those who depend on public transport for the journey to work. In some cases this involves setting aside hours to make a journey that would take minutes in a car. The pressure is even greater when the risk of arriving late jeopardizes already precarious employment situations (Grieco, 1995). If flexibility forms one basis of a politics of time, waiting is another.

All transportation systems involve waiting but again different social groups are variably willing or able to wait. In addition, there are striking differences between the conditions afforded by the VIP airport lounge and the uncovered, unsafe, unlit and 'non-smart' bus stop. Some transport systems demand more waiting than others but even within the same transport system there are big variations in the degree of time-dependence (charter air passengers versus frequent flyers). As Breedveld (1998) points out, an individual's 'time sovereignty' (control over temporal flexibility) is significantly determined by social factors, including especially education. For those lacking time sovereignty, the issue may not be one of fine-tuning travel times so as to avoid hot spots, but of lacking public transport connections at the times they need to travel (in the case of shift workers, cleaners and so on), or of having no temporal leeway at all. In such situations the coordination of their personal or household schedules with those of the transport infrastructure can be extremely problematic.

Spatial Dimensions

This lack of leeway, and of flexibility, also relates to households' location in space. Some transport hot spots, such as rush hours and places, stem from how travel comes to be locked in to people's patterns of life, rather in the way that technologies can get locked into certain social patterns that make new technologies impossible to develop (see Arthur, 1994, on the notion of path-dependency). There is a long-term 'household path-dependency'. In other words modal choices are not simply a matter of short-term calculation but are also the consequence of longer-term commitment and obligation. Household path-dependencies arise from living near (or far from) rail or road links, a feature that then binds household members to a range of other commitments, to travel to specific schools, shops, workplaces and so on.

Arrangements that 'lock' members of households into travelling to certain places at certain times collectively create the momentous ebbs and flows of people and machinery which define certain cities and towns and can make some such places seem unbearably congested. The social–spatial fragmentation trends mentioned above also knit together and consequently change the landscape of opportunity for mobility. Hence it is no longer the case that a family can escape household path-dependencies of the kind we have described by simply relocating to another area. Instead the changing nature of urban space dictates travel patterns necessary to secure access to facilities previously available locally.

The distribution and density of hot and cold spots of space and time (and the consequent patterning of mobility) seen from the perspective of the household have to do with two apparently contradictory dimensions, namely those of lock-in and path-dependency, and the availability of resources that permit flexibility.

In addition all mobilities to some extent necessitate immobilities. Immobilities occupy space and time and carry their own environmental consequences (Urry, 2003b). We distinguish two forms of immobility. Firstly, there are periods of storage, for example when cars are housed whilst not in motion. In many societies each car may 'own' two or more geographically distant parking places, one outside its home, the other at its place of work (with others outside third spaces). One consequence is that up to half the land in large urban centres is given over to car-only environments even though these are unoccupied for more than 50 per cent of the time. Secondly, mobility involves temporary moments of rest at traffic lights, roundabouts, jams and dropping off points. At each such moment cars (but also aeroplanes, buses and trains) take up space, burning fuel and producing carbon deposits as they wait to take off again.

There are thus specialized periods and places of infrastructural immobility, storage and temporary rest. Exactly how, when and where these take place is of immense social, economic and environmental consequence. This in turn relates to the manner in which time is organized, since the intersections of these periods and places facilitate or preclude the seamless mobilities of people, objects and equipment across time–space. These factors again contribute to a politics of mobility, one in which control over time and space varies for different actors to varying extents.

To summarize, differences in the spatial and temporal flexibilities and path-dependencies of individuals, households and transport systems themselves, combined with changing compulsions to proximity, all conspire to structure different social groups' experience of transport infrastructures.

ANALYSING TRANSPORT INFRASTRUCTURES

An adequate analysis of transport infrastructures requires understanding the social and temporal aspects of travel and of more obvious spatial arrangements and processes. But how might these ideas be used in practice, and how might we characterize these incredibly intricate conglomerations of machines, desires, people, flows and networks? As an opening comment, it is evident that any attempt to describe transport infrastructures and the mobilities they enable and manage can only ever provide a partial picture. That said, new strategies are needed to make sense of the social, temporal and spatial dimensions at stake.

One possibility is to define and distinguish between the hot and cold spots of space and time and to thereby reveal the relation between rush hours, rush places and calmer, less dense locations and times. Such a strategy has the further advantage of acknowledging the complex intersection of individual and collective systems of mobility. Figure 8.2 formalizes these elements together.

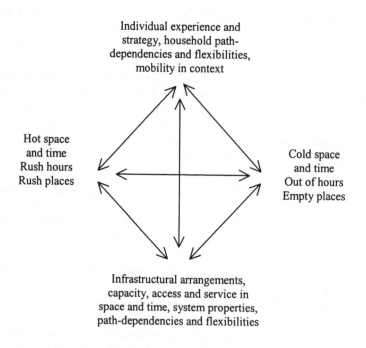

Figure 8.2 The individual and collective construction of 'hot' and 'cold' spaces and times

As this figure suggests, patterns of congestion and emptiness and of mobility and stasis (in space and time) are structured through the intersection between personal schedules and arrangements, and the infrastructures, resources and facilities available to those who travel. In order to understand the properties of the system as a whole we need to think about how, when and why combinations of people, proximity and conjunction get locked together. This means paying attention to the distribution of hot and cold spots of time and space, but above all to the relation between the hot and the cold both at the individual and at the aggregate levels. Furthermore the social framings and motivations of mobility must be borne in mind, from the grand social processes associated with globalization to the minutiae of individuals' and households' social obligations and compulsions to proximity. Yet the question remains, how might this be done in practice and what does our model imply for transport policy?

Guy et al. (1997) and Graham and Marvin (2001) provide some clues in their analyses of the hot and cold spots of urban form and of service provision (for example gas, electricity, telecommunications). Guy and Marvin (1996) point out that utility providers have concentrated on tailoring services for large-scale consumers, for example in the business zones of cities, often to the detriment of small-scale customers. Thus for a company consuming many thousands of units of water or electricity per day, special discounted unit rates are arranged and investment may be made to ensure an efficient, continuous supply. In another part of town, domestic consumers effectively subsidize these discounts and fund investment through higher service charges and unit rates. Similar processes are at work in transport provision.

Perhaps the best example of this in the UK was the programme of cuts applied to the railways in 1963 under Dr Beeching, in which 5000 miles of track and 2000 stations (almost a third of the entire network) were closed. The rationale then, as now, was to abandon loss-making lines and stations in order to capitalize on intercity routes, with profitability being the determining factor. Since privatization, bus and train companies have sought to streamline provision and focus on the major times and spaces of consumption.

In temporal terms, the modernist 'working day' also structures public transport provision with the result that periods before and after 8 am and 6 pm are frequently deserts of transport availability, the same being true of weekends and holidays.

Although shaped by other factors, the configuration of transport networks reveals a particular structuring of space and time. Careful reading of bus and train timetables might be used to identify 'hot' corridors and hubs surrounded by areas of 'cold'. Adding time to the picture we might imagine these hot zones as pulsing on and off in daily and weekly rhythms, with capillary structures (representing the connections available from transport corridors) bringing infrastructural 'heat' into the cold zones. Putting these ideas into action, and doing so for two locations in County Durham, we produced space–time maps of provision like the one shown in Figure 8.3 (see Cass et al., 2003, for more detail).

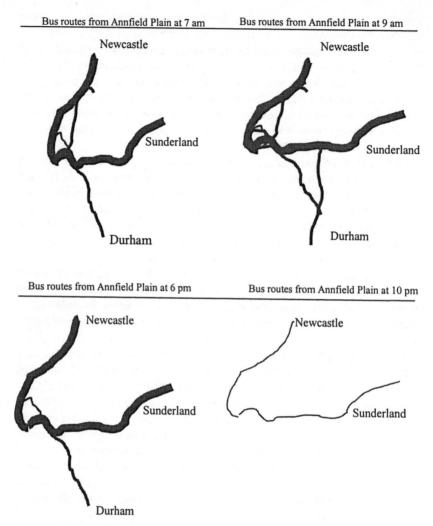

*Figure 8.3 Mapping bus routes from Annfield Plain in North East England
          in time and space*

These maps provide a striking visual representation of the dominance of
key routes and of the time-bounded nature of service provision. Consistent
with other empirical studies in West Newcastle and rural Lancashire (Cass et
al., 2003, Chapter 8) our mapping revealed a rather dramatic cut-off point at
around 6 pm. But as an exercise in capturing the spatial–temporal properties
of provision this analysis has a number of limitations. These are worth

describing in some detail for they point to important problems for social analysis and for policy.

The seemingly simple exercise of describing public transport provision proved to be almost impossibly challenging. Simply counting the number of buses leaving a specific location during the course of a day gives a sense of the temporal distribution of the service but tells us little of where these routes go. While it was possible to map the routes taken by all the buses that left a given stop (as in Figure 8.3), this makes no allowance for the fact that people can switch to another route, or transfer from bus to train (providing such options exist in space and time). Since we do not know where people actually go, we get no sense of the total journey times involved, or of the cost. Although we can describe and compare the number of buses per hour or the destinations that can be reached directly at different times of day, we cannot thereby conclude that the infrastructure is essentially richer in one area than in another.

No matter how we approach the problem, it is so far difficult to capture or represent the socio-spatial and temporal qualities of a transport infrastructure in a way that makes sense to those who use it. Other methodologies are of course possible. We might for instance turn our attention to actual users, following them as they move through time and space. While this would show how infrastructures are used in practice, it would not tell us much about the properties and qualities of the system as a whole and especially of what obligations to co-presence were not permitted at different times. After all, individuals only encounter those aspects that impinge on their ability (or otherwise) to make specific journeys.

Our provisional conclusion is that we need to find a way of revealing the properties of the physical–temporal infrastructure at a 'middle' level – that is at a level not so abstracted as to be of little practical relevance, but not so localized (such as the day-to-day experiences of actual travellers) as to require case-by-case surveying. Our representation of the social, spatial and temporal dimensions of mobility might be plausible and convincing at a general level but we have yet to operationalize these concepts in a way that describes actual systems of transport provision. This is important on two counts. It calls into question at least some of the necessarily loose generalizations on which much discussion is based. In addition the inability to capture the intersection of social, spatial and temporal dimensions suggests that transport policy-makers have no option but to work with simplified and predominantly spatial representations of the systems they seek to influence.

CONCLUSION

While we might not be able to represent the fabric of provision in great detail we can conclude by making some basic points. First, the future of transport infrastructures depends not only on the distribution of roads, railways, cars, buses, trains and so on but also on the structure and organization of social interactions. The relation between planning and transportation is already well known – what is missing, but what might be incorporated, is a more explicit recognition of the temporal dimension of social interactions. For the most part, Local Transport Plans in the UK (the basis of transport infrastructure improvement nationally) focus on space rather than time. Where they do deal with time they do so on the scale of minutes and journeys, not engaging with the more macro-level issues associated with the scheduling and coordination of the crucially significant social activities. By taking account of space and time, local authorities and others would be able to identify non-transport-related opportunities for intervention (most obviously through access-related initiatives) which have far-reaching effects on the mobility system as a whole.

Second, transport policies like those that promote car-sharing, lift-sharing and car-pooling, both require and engender new forms of temporal and spatial coordination. Difficulties in actually operating these schemes relate to some of the trends already identified: flexible working hours, increased commuting distances from scattered locations, and a valuing of travelling alone and at whim. In designing such schemes, the challenge is to tailor them to meet the specific demands of time–space coordination that people increasingly confront in their day-to-day lives. In this respect, 'demand responsive transport' (DRT) schemes have the important quality of addressing some of the temporal as well as spatial problems faced by those who depend on public transport. DRT buses that depart from timetables to service cold zones of service provision build in the spatial and temporal flexibility expected by car users and desired by others. In their operation they can simultaneously reveal and 'reheat' the cold zones of transport provision that are created (in part) by privatization and the pursuit of short-term commercial gain by operators.

Third, there are limits to local authorities' agency, not least because policies and schemes have timetables of their own. It can take years for urban and rural plans to really take effect and major investment in transport infrastructure is a long drawn out process. New ways of using existing systems (such as DRT) can sometimes be introduced at relatively short notice, yet infrastructures have self-fulfilling qualities and a reach and influence that go far beyond those anticipated by those who plan them.

Recognizing this last point is important for policy and practice. Just as the socio-technical infrastructures of the petroleum car have cast their long shadow over countless lives over the twentieth century, so systems laid down at the beginning of this new century may exert an irreversible force, shaped by but also shaping the social, temporal and spatial organization of everyday life for decades to come. This chapter has revealed just how intertwined social life is with complex times and spaces.

NOTE

1. Department of Sociology, Lancaster University. This chapter arises from a report produced for the CHIME project, CHanging Infrastructures, Measuring Exclusion, funded by the DfT 2002–3. The project explored how local authorities in the UK might model and assess transport-related social exclusion, especially in the context of the potential introduction of congestion charges, both road user charges and workplace parking levies (see Cass et al., 2003). The DfT is not responsible for the contents of this chapter. The chapter also benefits from discussions within CeMoRe, the Centre for Mobilities Research based at Lancaster University.

9. Infrastructures, crises and the orchestration of demand

Heather Chappells and Elizabeth Shove

INTRODUCTION

In August 2003, more than 50 million consumers in North America experienced power blackouts that brought cities including New York to a standstill (Barron, 2003; Semple and Barron, 2003). Thousands were stranded in lifts and on trains. At the same time, electrically operated pumping stations broke down, leaving many households without water. For three weeks during the winter of 1998, the central district of the city of Auckland in New Zealand was also without power – apartment blocks were evacuated, business ground to a halt and normal life was suspended (Hutton, 1998). During January 2001, California's electricity network reportedly 'ran out' of power (Cavanagh, 2002; Clark, 2001; Siohansi, 2002). In the UK, severe storms during the winters of 1995 and 1996 ravaged power lines in the North West of England, disrupting electricity supplies just as many families were sitting down to Christmas dinner. The following summer, rainfall levels in the same region dropped well below average for a prolonged period and many reservoirs dried up. As Hutton (1998) observes, events like these reveal the distinctive qualities of electricity and water: unlike designer dresses, where an interruption of supply poses few immediate consequences, energy and water are essential ingredients of modern life. Infrastructure system failure is an issue for everyone, not just shareholders.

Despite its tangible immediacy, the concept of failure deserves further attention. In the contexts considered here, failure means failure to maintain supply regardless of the ebb and flow of demand. Although energy experts disagree about the precise cause, there is general consensus that the extent of recent power failures in the USA related to the age of the electricity transmission and distribution system and a more endemic failure to 'keep up' with demand (Firestone and Pérez-Peña, 2003; Semple and Barron, 2003). In response, George Bush commented that this was a 'wake-up call' to modernize the nation's 'antiquated' grid (McDougall, 2003). Implicit in these accounts is the idea that infrastructure systems 'fail' when they fail to meet demand.

Because infrastructures have been designed around this notion of success and failure the strategy of (over)sizing to cope with peak demand is embedded in physical systems and in the operating principles of the companies involved. Maintaining a balance between supply and demand is however a continual achievement fraught with tension and uncertainty. In one of the cases we describe, reconfigured organizations struggle to control Victorian technologies in order to meet new patterns of demand. As we explain, socio-technical interdependencies of this kind are important both for the production of crises and for responses to them.

In taking forward these ideas, this chapter examines the naturalization of demand and its socio-technical construction at different points, both in time and in the supply chain. This is important, for the details of exactly how demand is made and met are of immediate consequence for the construction of infrastructures that are less vulnerable and at the same time more sustainable. Taking a longer-term perspective, present patterns of demand are not sustainable. By perpetuating them, and by planning to increase supply in order to avert short-term failure, infrastructure managers pave the way towards environmental crises of an altogether more global scale. As we hope to show, this need not be the only option.

By looking behind the scenes at the work involved in coordinating and scheduling flows of water and electricity in the UK, we show how the social and material features of existing networks generate moments of overloading, undercapacity and breakdown. As we also demonstrate, these same systems influence the demand or supply management strategies open to and adopted by consumers and providers. On the basis of this analysis, we argue that the development of more sustainable systems requires a new philosophy of provision and with it the renegotiation of consumption, production and demand. Critically, this does not depend upon the choices of individual end-consumers alone. In underlining the extent to which organizational and technological systems intersect, we argue that strategies for sustainability need to focus on the design and operation of entire systems of provision.

We begin with a brief discussion of the relation between consumption and production and the significance of storage and flow for the management of supply and demand. Although we identify general trends, the challenges involved in managing water and electricity differ on a number of important counts. Whereas water managers confront 'natural' variation in supply (drought and flood), electricity providers face problems of socio-spatial distribution within and between urban and rural areas. In looking at precisely how such challenges are managed, and how flows of water and electricity are 'orchestrated', we explore the qualities and properties of mainstream or 'mass' and marginal or 'niche' systems of provision. This exercise suggests that the scale of provision, and the socio-technical qualities of infrastructural systems, generate significantly different interpretations of demand and of success and failure.

CONSUMPTION AND PRODUCTION, STORAGE AND FLOW

Infrastructure planners routinely distinguish between supply and demand and between the activities of producers and the needs of their consumers. By contrast, writers like Fine and Leopold (1993) highlight systemic interactions between the worlds of consumption and production, showing how different actors along the supply chain jointly shape the possibilities and practices of demand and supply management. Implicit in such accounts is the idea that the activities of households and of utilities affect the operation of the grid that links them. These are not the only players involved. Although electricity and water supply are now framed by a political economy of privatization and although markets are liberalized, regulatory agencies set service standards that continue to inform the practicalities of supply and demand management.

Although Fine and Leopold (1993) focus on social organization, the relation between consumption and production is also mediated by complexes of material stuff. As Cass et al. suggest (this volume), cars, parking spaces and waiting rooms are important in permitting the movement of consumers, the operation of timetables and the scheduling of urban life. Questions of storage and flow are just as significant for electricity and water. For example the provision of a reliable electricity supply depends upon an organized sequence of sub-stations, transformers, wires and socket outlets. Although water is sometimes consumed direct from source, it is more usually channelled, contained and collected through a network of aqueducts, pipes, taps and sinks. In both cases, physical networks of storage and flow collectively 'script' the strategies and actions of the various system managers involved and of the consumers with whom they (and their technologies) interact.

As Hughes (1983) argues, social and technical systems are jointly implicated in processes of infrastructural development – and hence in the configuration of distinctive systems of provision. What he does not acknowledge is that certain forms of 'hardware' outlive the social and organizational concepts of which they were a part. One contemporary consequence is that modern managers are, to some extent, locked into modes of operation by the technologies they deal with. Writing of the UK, Patterson (2003) describes the result as a stultifying 'legacy mind-set', in which concepts belonging to previous eras of network construction – such as a 'predict and provide' logic – are embodied in the infrastructure itself, and continue to shape expectations about provision, consumption and the possibilities for demand management.

As indicated above, socially and technically viable strategies of demand management depend upon the intersection of organizational and technological systems. The material properties of the resources in question are also relevant. Compared to traffic systems, electricity and water networks are tightly coupled (Juhlin, 1994), being organized around connections that physically link consumers to providers. The 'tightness' of fit has important consequences for the operation of the system as a whole. Because electricity providers have to manage supply and demand in real time, networks of power have been designed to reach locations or users likely to generate 'desirable' load profiles – that is those that are optimal from the provider's point of view. Since water can be stored, management priorities are somewhat different. In this case, issues of quality and consistency determine the steps and stages of storage and flow and hence the moments and possibilities of demand management.

Existing infrastructures and material properties modify and mediate the effects of recent organizational restructuring. While it is true that previously homogeneous monopolies have been institutionally fragmented and unbundled (Graham and Marvin, 2001), there is some debate about what this means for the management of supply and demand. Awerbuch (2003) argues that there are now more options for 'just-in-time' energy production – and if suppliers can match demand as it occurs there should be less need for high safety margins or for spare plant or back-up storage facilities. Guy and Marvin (1996) suggest that institutional fragmentation has reconfigured priorities such that electricity customers in urban hot spots have suddenly become the focus of intensive load management programmes. On the other hand, Graham and Marvin (2001) doubt that new organizational arrangements will make much difference to the management of relatively stable assets and technologies. Further, Moss (in this volume) argues that competition in the water sector has proceeded relatively slowly precisely because of the difficulties of opening up spatially bound infrastructures to multiple distributors or suppliers.

In any event it is clear that the pace and direction of change vary across systems and do so in ways that reflect their social and material configuration. Just as important, and as illustrated by other contributors to this collection (see Van Vliet), privatization and liberalization have created 'spaces' in which novel systems of provision are emerging. Since the early 1990s new sub-systems and micro-grids have been developed alongside conventional arrangements (Van Vliet, 2002; Von Meier, 1994). In these niche situations, systems of storage and flow can be structured and balanced in ways that suit the social and environmental objectives of specific consumers and providers.

In the following sections we take a closer look at how utility managers in fact handle the day-to-day challenges of managing supply and demand. As well as showing what generic trends (like those of institutional fragmentation) mean in practice, this exercise illustrates the co-configuration of supply and demand and shows how this works out within mainstream or 'mass' and marginal or 'niche' systems of electricity and water provision.

MAINSTREAM SYSTEMS OF PROVISION

Interviews with distribution and supply managers (employed by United Utilities) provide revealing insights into the management of storage and flow and through that the balancing of supply and demand.[1] Their accounts of collecting, moving and allocating electricity and water give a sense of what is involved. The first case, based on the experiences of water managers in the North West of England, shows how distribution and supply technologies, including aqueducts or sub-stations, function as mediating devices, supporting and reinforcing some but not all forms of supply and demand management.

Managing Water

The history of Manchester's water supply can be traced back to the beginning of the sixteenth century, when a spring in Fountain Street was linked by aqueduct to an open conduit in the centre of the township, over a distance of half a mile or so. Pressure of demand led the Court Leet in 1578 to fix the daily ration per household to that which a woman could carry in a vessel on her head. By 1775 the spring had dried up and other local water sources were unable to meet growing need (Porter, 1978, p. 36).

Today, much of Manchester's water comes from reservoirs situated in the hills of the Lake District over 100 kilometres away, rather than from localized sources. The buckets and wells of the past have been replaced by a highly integrated supply infrastructure consisting of a sequence of storage reservoirs and aqueducts now managed by a large multinational utility company.[2] These highly integrated socio-technical arrangements have significant implications both for the sustainable allocation of water and for the alleviation of crises.

One of the distinctive technological features of the North West network is that much of its water is gravity-fed. Once released into an aqueduct that starts high in the Lake District, water gathers momentum and travels for great distances without the need for expensive mechanical pumping. This gravity-fed system, opened in 1894, is notoriously unresponsive, being described by one regional distribution manager as 'a slow cumbersome animal that is difficult to ramp up and down'. Technological arrangements of this kind have a powerful influence on the options available to those responsible for supplying water to the cities of North West England. In assessing how much water they need to meet demand in their designated patch, local supply managers observe current service reservoir levels and evaluate these against records of previous diurnal and annual variation. If deemed necessary, they request more resources from regional distribution managers higher up the supply chain. But as one regional manager explains, the business of allocating water is not entirely straightforward:

> It would be an extremely simple system if supply managers said they wanted another 10 megalitres to match demand, we would decide which button to press and out of the pipe came 10 megalitres. It doesn't work like that because we're built on the old gravity systems of the Victorians ... From Thirlmere to Manchester there's not one pump along it, so if you imagine it's almost like an open canal and if you put some more water on at Thirlmere it takes a day to get down to Manchester. So you imagine the guy in Manchester saying 'right I want a bit more water today he's got a day lag before he'll see it down there. If you try and work that tightly on the gravity aqueducts you'll be forever chasing a target you'll never achieve. I've got an analogy that it's not like firing a speedboat across a harbour, it's like sailing a huge oil tanker that you try and gently tease the system one way or another to meet demand as you'll never get in sync with it, you'll always be increasing when the guys are saying I want a reduction and you'll end up chasing the whole thing. (Extract from interview with Distribution Manager, United Utilities)

Given the delay in getting water to where it is needed, the decision to release water into the aqueduct is risky because, once moving downhill, the flow cannot be reversed. If anticipated demand fails to materialize, expensively treated water must be diverted to another suitable location. Failing that, it will be flushed away before even reaching the end-consumer.

This example illustrates the balancing of supply and demand in a centralized system of distribution and management. In this case, the infrastructure itself influences the strategies and practices of those who manage it. Regional distribution managers consequently find themselves working with a system that is fundamentally unresponsive and quite out of step with current ideas about network efficiency and 'just-in-time' management.

At the same time, regional water managers have to meet new standards of security and service. Between the months of April 1995 and October 1996, the North West received an unprecedented 17 months of below-average rainfall and went from being one of the wettest regions in the country to one of the driest. During this time many of the major strategic reservoirs designed to provide continuous water supply to the region's users virtually dried up. Following the drought, regional distribution managers came under pressure from the regulator to review their policy on supply security. The company is now expected to survive the worst drought ever and maintain river margins without the use of emergency storage systems. These requirements mean that the company has to keep more 'headroom' in the system than ever before.[3] As a result the allowable yield (the amount of water that managers have available for consumers) across the regional system has effectively dropped from 2600 megalitres to 2200 megalitres a day. Although the technical infrastructure is unchanged, a new 'virtual' ceiling has been imposed. As the modification of headroom indicates, it is possible to set new demand ceilings within an integrated water system providing these are lower than those literally built into the technical fabric of aqueducts and storage reservoirs.

Water managers' experiences highlight two important features of infrastructural orchestration. First, they show the socio-technical system of water provision to be both durable and flexible. Although the system has been subject to new demands (like those following the 1995–96 drought) and new forms of organization, other features (like the gravity-fed aqueduct) remain steadfastly in place. The second related point is that change of any kind is significant for storage, flow and the daily management of supply and demand. Although it is usual to suppose that systems are designed to meet pre-existing patterns of demand, the reverse is also the case: in other words, concepts of 'proper provision' are engendered and reproduced through the day-to-day operation of the network as a whole.

Arguments about the obduracy of certain organizational concepts are also relevant to understanding the contemporary management of regional electricity networks. Rather than repeating the points made above, we use the case of electricity to explore the social and spatial aspects of infrastructural provision and their implications for strategies of demand, or more commonly, supply management.

Managing Electricity

At the turn of the nineteenth century, electricity in the UK was provided by a patchwork of local networks each constructed and operated by independent public and private suppliers with little external regulation or centralized control (Frost, 1993). Nowadays the map of electricity provision is radically different. In North West England just one company (United Utilities) is responsible for distributing electricity to more than 2 million customers along a highly interconnected network, comprising many hundreds of kilometres of overhead and underground power lines. The task of 'regional load coordination' falls to network managers located at the control centre in Manchester. By recording and mapping the load status of the entire distribution system these managers identify load-related problems on the network and coordinate a response. As they explain, the system is configured with high levels of technical interconnection and duplication. This means that there are many opportunities for rerouting electricity between different parts of the network. Exactly which strategy is adopted, which route is taken and when, depend in turn on a range of other considerations having to do with the intensity and timing of loads and the status of the existing infrastructure at particular locations.

In some places, like the city centre of Manchester, capacity is already stretched. New commercial and residential developments and anticipated load growth mean that the city is the biggest 'hot spot' in the North West. In response, United Utilities has established a specialist connections team, charged with the task of organizing the network so as to meet the needs of all these new users. This typically involves asking property developers to say how much additional load they expect to require and then figuring out how these extra megawatts might be delivered, either by tweaking the network or by extending it, for instance by building new sub-stations.

Quite different strategies are adopted when dealing with locations on the periphery of the network. In rural areas consumers tend to be served by overhead lines. These are especially vulnerable to breakdown and, since they are quite literally at the end of the line, there is often little scope for the substitution of loads.[4] Regional managers explained how difficult it was (in a privatized system) to justify investment in these areas.[5] Certainly the economics are quite unlike those involved in reinforcing the network in central Manchester. However, the management of supply and demand remains a political as well as an economic issue, as illustrated by the company's response to storm damage experienced during the winters of 1998 and 1999. Severe storm conditions brought down overhead lines, resulting in widespread power cuts across large parts of Cumbria and the Lake District over two consecutive Christmas periods. Faced with public and regulatory pressure in response to what was seen as the 'mismanagement' of its network, United Utilities has since implemented plans that will see several millions of pounds of investment being pumped into these network 'cold spots'. As this example illustrates, the legacy of public ownership, supported by current regulatory systems and the weight of consumer expectation (especially about security of supply), continues to exert a powerful influence, prompting investment in locations in which it is not 'economically' justified:

If the lights go out for half an hour you might curse but if it's back in half-an-hour it's no big deal is it, but if it's off for 20 hours you're going to start getting upset aren't you ... it depends when it is, I mean if it goes off in the middle of the night you're not going to be bothered are you, but if you're in the middle of cooking the Christmas dinner... (Extract from interview with Distribution Manager, United Utilities)

Although Guy and Marvin (1996) anticipate increasing differentiation between the management of hot and cold spots (the former being the subject of intensive demand management and the latter the scene of strategic withdrawal), our research tells another story. In Manchester city centre, an area of significant load growth, distribution managers adopted a hands-off approach to demand management, falling back on conventional supply-building strategies. Meanwhile in rural Cumbria, an area of dispersed load and few customers, the utility is investing in real-time monitoring equipment designed to improve levels of interconnection and minimize interruptions to supply and distribution losses.

In discussing methods of hot and cold spot management electricity managers highlight the importance of maintaining supply to users. In practice, strategies for alleviating load-related problems vary depending on network location, and on the overall load profile of the region. However, the overall story remains one of investment in supply rather than management of demand.[6]

Questions of social, spatial and temporal distribution and of storage and flow take different forms with respect to electricity and water. But in both cases, the overriding ethos is one of meeting what are taken to be non-negotiable consumer 'needs'. This is so despite the fact that managers are themselves aware of how much work is involved in juggling and in a sense constructing, anticipating and effectively co-producing demand through the detailed design and operation of the infrastructures with which they are involved.

MARGINAL SYSTEMS OF PROVISION

In the situations described above, the logic of infrastructural development is one of mass production characterized by heavyweight centres of provision in the form of reservoirs and aqueducts, power stations and national grids. This section considers other ways of managing water and electricity and of orchestrating supply and demand. The examples described represent extreme situations in which households and communities construct and operate their own 'mini-grids', often disconnected from mainstream networks.

In the UK a number of sustainable housing schemes, mostly initiated during the early 1990s, have sought to achieve some level of autonomy from mainstream infrastructures.[7] The Hockerton Housing Project, developed by five households in Nottinghamshire, exemplifies this approach. Instead of relying on mainstream electricity supply, homes are designed to capture solar energy and store this in the form of heat around the building. These passive architectural features should keep householders warm during all but the coldest periods. Elsewhere, three households in the Allerton Park development in Leeds have established an on-site water network, incorporating drinking and grey-water supply, again designed as a stand-alone system disconnected from the regional utility's network.

In these two cases, the highly localized nature of energy and water provision means that balances between system capacity and demand are typically tight and unpredictable. Self-providers' ability to heat their homes or run the tap depends on recent weather patterns – including levels of rainfall or hours of sunshine. The households involved have developed a distinctive approach to demand management, arranging a variety of routines around the availability of resources that most of us take for granted. In Hockerton, rather than building system capacity capable of dealing with extreme loads (as is common practice in mainstream grids), households adopt a range of demand management strategies, putting on extra clothes during cooler weather and taking fewer showers if that is what is needed to 'flatten' peak load and keep supply systems in balance.

The extent to which localized management strategies of this kind work depends on a variety of factors, including the duration and frequency of supply interruption, and the definition of needs that must be met. For water self-providers in Leeds, the problems of balancing supply and demand on such a small scale came to a head one winter when their private water supply froze. Faced with the prospect of going without water, two of the three households reconnected to the mains. Households at Hockerton have also renegotiated their relationship with mainstream electricity providers in order to secure back-up heating systems for especially cold nights. After rejecting the use of diesel generators on environmental grounds, and running into planning opposition for a proposed wind turbine, Hockerton's residents opted for mains electricity to boost indoor temperatures during winter.

As these examples show, marginal utility managers (that is consumers and households) face distinctive challenges in coordinating the spatial and temporal flow of resources and in managing micro-systems of supply and demand. In these situations the distinction between provider and consumer collapses, opening up new opportunities for the coordination of demand and supply and for the 'real-time' management of resources and resource-consuming activities. Each of the marginal arrangements we have described brings with it a unique set of options for juggling production and consumption. At the same time, the social and technical viability of new modes of organization and of associated operating principles varies depending on how well they mesh with mainstream arrangements – including existing infrastructures (for example the cost or possibility of back-up grid connection) and associated regulatory standards (for example of water quality or planning).

The experiences of those operating niche or marginal infrastructures help expand our understanding of the relation between supply and demand. The challenges of managing storage and flow between a handful of households are quite unlike those faced by United Utilities. Although the close coupling of supply and demand is likely to be more sustainable than the unending strategy of predict and provide, we do not argue that 'small is beautiful' or that self-provision is inherently 'better'. The point is to see what lessons these admittedly extreme cases of niche provisioning hold for mainstream providers.

ORCHESTRATING DEMAND

In switching between examples relating to water and electricity networks and in considering mainstream and marginal scales of provision, we make the point that forms of flexibility and responsiveness vary widely. Regional distribution managers' accounts of the challenges involved in mainstream water provision show how technical infrastructures influence the balancing of supply and demand across the system as a whole. Technologies, including aqueducts but also overhead power lines, constitute forms of 'connective tissue' binding consumers and providers together and locking both into distinctive regimes of resource management. Examples of mainstream electricity provision illustrate the social and institutional importance of maintaining supply, and show the different logics that underpin investment in reinforcement and additional capacity with regard to hot and cold spots in the network.

These cases show that the intensity and scope of demand management are highly variable and related to formal and informal obligations and to technical standards and expectations of service, as well as to the ceilings set and the possibilities afforded by different technological arrangements. They also show that the dominant logic remains one of reactive and incremental expansion, reinforcement and interconnection. Given this orientation, it is perfectly reasonable for distribution and supply managers to want to upgrade antiquated grids in order to avoid breakdown and failure. On the other hand, and from an environmental perspective, it is important to ask whether this supply-side model of network modernization is ultimately sustainable and whether a more radical reassessment of service expectation and provision is required.

Consideration of the orchestration of supply and demand management at the margins of provision suggests that infrastructures can be reconfigured in ways that challenge the dominant mindset. Self-providers cope with periods of intermittent supply by adjusting their clothing or rescheduling their activities, thereby challenging the idea that electricity or water supply has to be continuously and instantaneously available around the clock. The extent to which households adapt depends, in part, on the duration of disruption to 'normal' service, the back-up systems available and their perception of 'normality'. In the cases we studied, various thresholds were reached. Having discovered points beyond which they were unwilling to go, households at Hockerton and at Allerton Park renegotiated their personal and collective dependencies on the mains grid, opting for reconnection in order to meet peak-time demand or to manage emergencies. These experiences raise a number of more general questions about how expectations and conventions become normalized and about the circumstances under which people renegotiate practices and routines like those of bathing, cooking or heating (Shove, 2003).

These extreme arrangements are instructive on a number of counts. As already mentioned, they challenge the notion that continual, universal provision of water and electricity is the only goal. Just as important, they illustrate ways of combining niche and mass systems of provision. For the residents of Hockerton and Allerton Park, mainstream and marginal systems figure as complementary rather than alternative modes of provision. Further questions arise about whether and how such combinations might be managed on any scale, but these are questions already being asked by those interested in the longer-term future of ageing grids and rusting pipes, and in the possibilities of developing much more decentralized networks (especially of power).

In thinking about these and other options, it is important to acknowledge the flexibility and obduracy of existing socio-technical arrangements. In showing how these structure opportunities for demand management (not in principle, but in detail), the rather pragmatic point that concepts of success, failure and demand are built into the hardware and into the organizational mindsets of which infrastructures are constituted is demonstrated. The continuing influence of the Thirlmere aqueduct illustrates this rather clearly. However, current forms of investment, for instance in Manchester city centre or in Cumbria, have consequences of their own – in their different ways both structure possibilities and constrain options for the utility managers of the future.

Under current conditions it is likely that networks will be modernized in ways that perpetuate supply-oriented strategies and the mindsets and technologies associated with them. If the risks of long-term environmental crises are to be reduced, other approaches will be needed. These will almost certainly require a fundamental reassessment of underlying philosophies and practices of infrastructure provision. Such strategies might involve constructing (or reconstructing) infrastructure systems around principles of interrupted rather than continual supply. Mass and niche systems of provision might be combined to form new configurations of central and local supply and correspondingly novel ways of conceptualizing and managing base and peak loads. The experiences of those managing marginal systems suggest that infrastructures can be managed and manipulated on different scales. Likewise the experiences of mainstream providers show that existing infrastructures can be operated and managed in significantly different ways should organizational priorities and procedures change. Utilities might for instance extend the use of contracts in which consumers are explicitly enrolled as the co-managers of demand.

Something of this kind may happen not for long-term environmental reasons but because ageing infrastructures are, in any event, running into limits of their own. As utility managers warn, more frequent power cuts and water shortages are likely to result from increasing demand and reduced levels of spare capacity. Faced with imminent 'failure', the challenge is to develop solutions that do not follow the 'natural' trajectory of incremental expansion and capacity-building. This is important, for there is the very real possibility that far from being a way out, this route leads to 'failure' of a different kind.

NOTES

1. These 'mainstream' accounts are based on interviews undertaken as part of postgraduate study funded by the UK Economic and Social Research Council (see Chappells, 2003, ESRC award number: R00429934082). In the water sector, interviewees included managers at United Utilities (previously North West Water) responsible for the regional distribution of resources and those responsible for supplying water to consumers in specific demand management zones. In the electricity sector, network managers at United Utilities (previously Norweb Distribution) responsible for the coordination, connection and daily management of loads across the region were interviewed, along with those responsible for the connection of loads in urban 'hot spots' and for load-related reinforcement in rural 'cold spots'.
2. United Utilities was created in 1996 from the acquisition by North West Water plc (privatized in 1989) of Norweb plc (privatized in 1990). The company was the UK's first multi-utility, providing water, electricity, gas and telecommunications services.
3. 'Headroom' is a theoretical factor used by managers to assess the difference between the water available for use and final demand.

4. This is a particular problem in the North West, with about 75 per cent of the regional network consisting of overhead lines compared to a national average of 60 per cent (Norweb Distribution, 1998).
5. Security-of-supply performance indicators (set by the UK electricity regulator OFGEM) have traditionally been based on the number of customers affected when things go wrong. This has meant that for many UK electricity companies, investments in urban hot spots with high consumer densities were a priority.
6. During 1999–2000 United Utilities spent in the region of £40 million on 'load-related investment', defined as those activities that extend and increase the capacity of the network (Norweb Distribution, 2000).
7. Interviews with the initiators of the Hockerton Housing Project and the Allerton Park Housing Development were undertaken as part of the European Union-funded Domus project (EU DGXII 1997–2000, award number: ENV-CT97-0467) – see Chappells et al. (2000).

10. Conclusions

Heather Chappells, Bas Van Vliet and Dale Southerton

The contributions to this collection have introduced new dimensions to debates about the organization of sustainable consumption that have been overlooked or marginalized in the existing environmental policy literature. Most significantly, they have positioned consumption, and hence opportunities for environmental action, in the context of specific modes and systems of service provision. Whether consumers are able to contribute to the development of more sustainable systems of provision depends on how they are socially situated and on the socio-technical systems to which they are attached. Furthermore, consumer and provider perceptions of what constitutes 'sustainable' consumption are highly interpretative, context-dependent and open to negotiation over time.

These arguments have been developed, tested and reframed with reference to rapidly changing landscapes of infrastructure provision: environments in which new configurations of players, socio-technical constellations and logics of service provision are emerging alongside more traditional arrangements. In viewing consumption within this dynamic context, it has been possible to challenge the dominant view that individuals are the key to sustainable provision. Although a limited notion of consumer choice undoubtedly has a part to play in shaping more sustainable systems of provision, the explanatory value of this concept is weakened once account is taken of the extent to which utilities, intermediaries and infrastructures together with the conventions and routines of daily practices configure the options available to individuals.

Another advantage in focusing on these utility sectors has been to show how the character of the commodities at stake is critical in framing patterns of consumption and opportunities for environmental reform. The everyday services provided through energy, water, transport or waste networks cannot be analysed in the same terms as those items purchased over a shop counter. In this respect the contributions to this volume challenge a resource-based paradigm that deals in bundles of homogeneous commodities. Together they show how goods and services are the products of specific historical, institutional and social systems that shape service expectations, daily practices and associated patterns of resource use. This conclusion summarizes the main themes to emerge from the volume and how the insights generated might inform a more socio-structural perspective on sustainable consumption.

SUSTAINABLE CONSUMPTION: EMERGING THEMES

In reviewing the chapters, four cross-cutting themes can be identified that help us to understand the character of sustainable consumption in infrastructures of provision.

Consumer–Provider Interdependencies and the Structuring of Choice

In the first part of this book, Southerton et al. and Spaargaren offered two different perspectives on the extent to which consumption can be thought of as a socially negotiated enterprise framed by the interdependency between consumers and providers. Critical questions about the relationships between consumption, lifestyle and choice that have been at the heart of environmental policy debates were addressed. Under what conditions are different groups of consumers able to make lifestyle choices? How are these choices constrained by social expectations and institutional rules or regulations? How willing or able are people to act as environmentally motivated citizen-consumers? Do people actually view their everyday consumption of environmental resources or services in terms of choice at all, or as a matter of routine, habit or social convention?

In exploring these issues, both sets of authors touched upon classic sociological debates concerning the relation between structure and agency in influencing human action, and about the extent to which consumption is a routine or reflexive enterprise (Bourdieu, 1984; Featherstone, 1991a; Giddens, 1991a; Beck et al., 1994; Gronow and Warde, 2001). For Spaargaren, it is less individual consumers' attitudes and behaviour that should be at the core of analysis and more the social practices that result from both consumer and producer actions. The process of reducing the environmental impacts of consumption should be analysed in terms of deliberate achievements of knowledgeable and capable agents who make use of the possibilities offered to them in the context of specific systems of provision. In such a view there are certainly individual possibilities towards environmental social change, but these depend on the levels and modes of 'green' provisioning.

Southerton et al. presented another argument. They suggested that even if consumers have a highly developed sense of social or environmental responsibility as well as access to the resources to pursue greener lifestyles, it does not necessarily follow that individual consumers autonomously engage in sustainable consumption. Critical to their argument is the suggestion that consumption occurs in order that people can competently engage in social practices. Practices are embedded in routine and normative ways of 'doing' social life, and interlock in ways that configure the possibilities for social change in what and how people consume. Despite differences in orientation and approach, both sets of authors suggest that understanding consumption solely as a matter of choice is inappropriate, especially in situations where consumers are connected to socio-collective material systems that lock them into certain service regimes.

The inappropriateness of choice is a theme taken up by Summerton, who reflects upon the construction of new service regimes in the energy sector. Within a free market ideology, the restructuring of utility systems is associated with an enlarged landscape of opportunity and choice for consumers, including the ability to select between different sorts of providers and specialized products. In reality the rhetoric of choice is loaded with paradoxes and contradictions. Although some consumers may be offered improved service options there is also an underclass of utility consumers, the low-income or fuel-poor, for whom the reverse is the reality. One of the most striking paradoxes is that although privatization and market liberalization claim to offer consumers more choice than ever before, it is utility companies that are 'choosing' their consumers and the service options available to them. Further exploration of contemporary energy service provision across Europe reveals disjunctures between the rhetoric and reality of market and environmental reform for many domestic consumers.

Intermediary Arrangements and New Spaces for Consumption

The second part of the volume drew attention to the importance of intermediary arrangements in shaping contexts for sustainable consumption. For Marvin and Medd, intermediaries represented strategic actors responsible for creating new 'spaces' for consumption and for environmental action between the spheres of consumption and provision. Meanwhile Van Vliet observed that the construction of a variety of intermediate scales of network organization is creating multiple opportunities for consumers and providers to create and configure more sustainable systems of service provision.

Yet the extent to which new intermediaries or intermediate scales of provision are contributing to the development of more sustainable patterns of consumption is still unclear. In many cases it appears that the scope for consumers to engage in new intermediary spaces of consumption or provision is highly differentiated and depends on the availability of localized support networks. Even in situations where highly environmentally motivated citizens have attempted to develop greener utility service regimes, they are often thwarted by institutionalized and normalized rules concerning acceptable modes of provision. Taking these cases into account, it appears that the promise of new intermediary arrangements in providing spaces for sustainable consumption has yet to be fulfilled.

Infrastructural Legacies and the Reproduction of Service Regimes

Several authors emphasized the interplay between infrastructural flexibility and inflexibility in structuring systems of consumption and provision. Decisions about travel or about the distribution, use or disposal of water, energy or waste depend on the configuration of technical networks and on the organizational principles or socio-technical scripts they embody. For example Chappells and Shove describe how patterns of resource use are mediated through technologies of storage and flow, which create certain opportunities for the coordination of demand across the system as a whole. Sometimes infrastructural legacies can prove especially intransigent or obdurate, to the extent that definitions of sustainable consumption might need to be reassessed. For example Moss argues that while the overconsumption of natural resources can be understood as an environmental and social 'bad', for contemporary utility managers, the technical legacy they have inherited means that underconsumption can also prove unsustainable in terms of the efficiency of the system as a whole.

Complex Systems of Provision and the Dynamics of Demand

Finally, the contributors to this volume support the idea that consumption must be treated as a systemic process involving multiple supply chain agencies rather than treated as the outcome of aggregated decisions made by autonomous individuals or households. To date, much environmental policy geared towards the utility sectors has focused on the extremes of supply chains – on the supply side the development of renewable generation, and the promotion of end-user efficiencies on the demand side. As Chappells and Shove argued, this approach overlooks the extent to which actors involved in the distribution and supply of resources can influence the volume and timing of resource flows and the orchestration of demand. Or, from the perspective of Cass et al., how 'hot' and 'cold' spaces of consumption are individually and collectively constructed. This theme of systemic interconnectivity is developed further by Moss, who argues that the organization of utility infrastructures needs to be seen in the context of the restructuring of entire urban environments. These contributions suggest that understanding overall patterns of resource use and regimes of service provision in utility systems requires analytical approaches that reconnect the activities of end-users to what goes on in the 'organizational middle' of networks, and how these activities connect to financial or political systems at large.

Together this collection of chapters suggests that to understand sustainable consumption in relation to changing infrastructures of provision it is necessary to:

- rethink concepts of choice in the context of arguments about the embedded, routine and interconnected basis of social practices, and the ideological construction of 'the consumer' and 'service options';
- take into account the role of social and technical intermediaries and how they reshape contexts for environmental action at different scales of organization;
- appreciate the extent to which infrastructural legacies continue to reinforce or reproduce certain practices and patterns of demand;
- recognize that consumption patterns and practices are dependent on the organization of specific systems of service provision and how they interface with other regimes of everyday life.

INFRASTRUCTURES AND SUSTAINABLE CONSUMPTION: REORIENTING THE AGENDA

On the basis of the arguments presented, it appears that understanding consumption in terms of individual choice has only limited explanatory value. Many of the services associated with energy and water provision are routinized to the extent that people rarely think about the consequences of their actions. In this context it is more relevant to consider how routines and habits are formed, how people come to expect certain levels of service provision and how these expectations might be uprooted.

In reviewing contemporary infrastructure arrangements, it also makes sense to understand consumption as a dynamic process shaped by relations between consumers, producers and intermediaries. It is the interface between these groups that defines a particular consumption 'space' and how different consumers are able to act within that space.

When applied to the utility sectors, consumption can also be understood as a socially and technically constructed phenomenon. Technologies are not only enrolled to fix end-user behaviour, they are also implicated in structuring relations between consumers and providers, configuring and supporting certain service regimes, and coordinating patterns of resource flow and use.

Thinking along these lines implies a shift away from the individualistic and resource-based paradigm of sustainable consumption which dominates current environmental research and policy approaches. Together the ideas and arguments expressed in this volume imply a reorientation in the analysis of sustainable consumption which accounts for:

- differentiated services and service regimes rather than homogeneous resources and generic market rules;
- consumers as social and collectively organized beings rather than as autonomous individuals or rational economic actors;
- technologies and institutions as the constructors and mediators of relations between consumers and systems of provision rather than as barriers or fixes;
- multidimensional modes and scales of organization that can configure different opportunities for environmental action;
- demand as something structured and orchestrated in socio-technical systems of provision rather than as something driven by market forces.

Analyses of the organization and operation of contemporary utility infrastructures have served to show how patterns of consumption are related to specific service regimes, scales of socio-technical organization and modes of provision. In these accounts attention has been drawn to the interfacing of old and new arrangements and what this means for the structuring and reproduction of certain consumption patterns and routines. In turn, these arrangements influence how meanings of sustainability are being renegotiated in practice.

Although meanings and practices of sustainable consumption are highly variable and dependent on the system or scale in question, it is possible to identify some of the core concepts that define the character of the socio-technical interactions at play. First, consumers and providers do not operate in autonomous spheres but are involved in the mutual negotiation of consumption and demand – what might usefully be thought of in terms of co-provision. Second, in the context of utility restructuring, it is important to understand how relationships between consumers and providers are changing, and to appreciate how new intermediaries are reframing contexts for action. These concepts might form the basis for a reorientation in approaches to the interpretation and analysis of sustainable consumption.

The challenge that changing infrastructural arrangements present for the sustainability agenda is also one of recognizing and fully appreciating the part played by existing systems of provision in structuring consumption and the detail of daily social practices. As the contributors to this volume have shown, utility consumers have only limited opportunities to significantly reconfigure their own individual routines of consumption. Another way of advancing the agenda on sustainable consumption, and one aptly demonstrated here, is to pay attention to the ways in which socio-technical and market regulatory arrangements at the systemic level further opportunities for the gradual reorientation of consumption habits across social groups and over time.

AFTERWORD

At the winter workshop that inspired this collection we asked participants to write limericks that captured the spirit of the event. It seems appropriate to end with the winning contribution:

They say there's no choice but to choose,
A claim that's designed to confuse,
But modes of provision
And social division
Are superior concepts to use.
(Palmer, Shove, Southerton and Warde, 2000)

Bibliography

Adam, B. (1990), *Time and Social Theory*, Philadelphia, PA: Temple University Press.

Adam, B. (1995), *Timewatch*, Cambridge: Polity.

Adam, B. (1998), *Timescapes of Modernity: The Environment and Invisible Hazards*, London, New York: Routledge.

Adams, J. (1999), *The Social Implications of Hypermobility*, OECD Project on Environmentally Sustainable Transport, Paris: OECD.

Akrich, M. (1992), 'The de-scription of technical objects', in W. Bijker, E. Wiebe and J. Law (eds), *Shaping Technology/Building Society. Studies in Sociotechnical Change*, Cambridge, MA: MIT Press.

Arthur, B. (1994), *Increasing Returns and Path Dependence in the Economy*, Ann Arbor, MI: University of Michigan Press.

Awerbuch, S. (2003), 'Decentralized Electricity Networks, Mass-Customization and Intermittent Renewables in the 21st Century: Taking a Giant Step Backwards', draft paper for Tyndall Centre Seminar on the Decarbonisation of Modern Societies, 22 October, UMIST.

Axhausen, K. (2002), 'Social networks and travel behaviour', ESRC Mobile Network Workshop, Cambridge, February.

B.& A Groep (2000), *Burger en Milieu. Verslag van een verkenning naar de potentie en meerwaarde van 'burger en milieu'* [Citizens and the environment. Exploring the potentials of a citizen-based approach to environmental policy-making], Hoofdrapport, Den Haag: VROM.

Ball, P. (1999) *H₂O: A Biography of Water*, London: Phoenix.

Bargeman, B. (2001), *Kieskeurig Nederland* [The Choosey Dutchman]: *Routines in the Holiday Choice of Dutch Tourists*, dissertation, Tilburg: Tilburg University.

Barron, J. (2003), 'Midday shutdowns disrupt millions', *New York Times*, 15 August.

Bauman, Z. (1983), 'Industrialism, consumerism and power', *Theory, Culture and Society*, 1 (3), 32–43.

Bauman, Z. (1988), *Freedom*, Milton Keynes: Open University Press.

Bauman, Z. (2000), *Liquid Modernity*, Cambridge: Polity Press.

Beck, U., A. Giddens and S. Lash (1994), *Reflexive Modernization*, Cambridge: Polity Press.

Beckers, T., P. Ester and G. Spaargaren (1999) (eds), *Verklaringen van duurzame consumptie; Een speurtocht naar nieuwe aanknopingspunten voor milieubeleid* [Explaining sustainable consumption; in search of new perspectives for environmental policy-making], Publicatiereeks Milieustrategie **10**, Den Haag: VROM.

Beckers, T., G. Spaargaren and B. Bargeman (2000), *Van gedragspraktijk naar beleidspraktijk; een analytisch instrument voor een consument-georiënteerd milieubeleid* [From social practice to policy practice: the social practices model as an analytic instrument for consumer-oriented environmental politics], Publicatiereeks milieustrategie **8**, Den Haag: VROM.

Berliner Wasserbetriebe (1997), *Geschäftsbericht* [Annual Report] *1996*, Berlin.

Bewag (Berliner Kraft- und Licht Aktiengesellschaft) (1995), *Geschäftsbericht* [Annual Report] *1994/95*, Berlin.

Bewag (Bewag Aktiengesellschaft) (2001), *Geschäftsbericht [Annual Report]* 2000/2001, Berlin.

Bladh, M. (2002), *En elektrisk historia: elsystemets och elanvändningens utveckling i Sverige*, working paper 247, Linköping University, Sweden, Department of Technology and Social Change.

Bladh, M. (2003), *Synpunkter på elmarknaden,* working paper, Linköping University, Sweden.

Blaza, A., S. Horrax and H. Hurt (2002), *'It's your choice! Influencing more sustainable patterns of production and consumption in the UK'*, report on a multi-stakeholder process by Imperial College London and UNED-UK Committee, July (www.env.ic.ac.uk/research/epmg/SPCP.html).

Blok, K. and K. Vringer (1995), *Energie-intensiteit van levensstijlen* (Energy-intensity of lifestyles), Utrecht: Vakgroep Natuurwetenschap en Samenleving.

Boardman, B. and T. Fawcett (2002), 'Competition for the Poor – liberalisation of electricity supply and fuel poverty: lessons from Great Britain for Northern Ireland', Environmental Change Institute, University of Oxford, unpublished.

Boden, D. and H. Molotch (1994), 'The compulsion to proximity', in R. Friedland and D. Boden (eds), *Now/Here. Time, Space and Modernity*, Berkeley, CA: University of California Press.

Bos, W. (2001), Public lecture by Secretary of State Wouter Bos on the significance of green taxes on behalf of the Ministry of Financial Affairs in the Netherlands, Wageningen, 19 February.

Bourdieu, P. (1984), *Distinction: A Social Critique of Judgement and Taste,* London: Routledge.

Bourdieu, P. (1997), 'The focus of social capital', in D. Halsey, P. Brown and A. Wells (eds), *Education, Culture, Economy, Society*, Oxford: Oxford University Press.

Bowker, G. and S.L. Star (1999), *Sorting Things Out: Classification and its Consequences*, Cambridge, MA: MIT Press.

Breedveld, K. (1998), 'The double myth of flexibilization: trends in scattered work hours, and differences in time sovereignty', *Time and Society*, 7, 129–43.

Brown, P. and L. Cameron (2000), 'What can be done to reduce overconsumption?', *Ecological Economics*, **32** (1), 27–41.

Brundtland (1987), *Our Common Future*, World Commission on Environment and Development, Oxford: Oxford University.

Burg, S., G. Spaargaren and A. Mol (2001), 'Environmental Monitoring: opportunities and threats of a consumer-oriented approach', paper presented at the ISA conference New Natures, New Cultures, New Technologies, Cambridge University, July.

Bushman, R. and C. Bushman (1988), 'The early history of cleanliness in America', *Journal of American History*, **74** (4), 1213–38.

Callon, M. (1997), 'Techno-economic networks and irreversibility', in J. Law (ed.), *A Sociology of Monsters: Essays on Power, Technology and Domination*, Sociological Review Monograph, London: Routledge.

Callon, M. (1998), *The Laws of the Market*, Sociological Review Monograph Series, Oxford: Blackwell.

Campbell, C. (1998), 'Conceiving consumption: a survey of the frames of meaning commonly employed in the study of consumption', paper presented at seminar on Consumption, Environment and Social Sciences, Oxford Centre for the Environment, Ethics and Society, Mansfield College, July.

Cass, N. (2002), 'Time thoughts: temporalities, time politics and exclusion', Lancaster University Sociology Department, unpublished.

Cass, N., E. Shove and J. Urry (2003), *Changing Infrastructures, Measuring Social–Spatial Inclusion/Exclusion*. Lancaster: Lancaster University Sociology Department and DfT.

Cavanagh, R. (2002), 'California overcomes an energy crisis', *Electricity Journal*, January/February, 92–3.

CEA (1999), *Minder energiegebruik door een andere leefstijl?* (Using less energy by a change of life-style?), Eindrapportage Project Perspectief, Den Haag: Ministerie van VROM.

Chappells, H. (2003), 'Re-conceptualising electricity and water: institutions, infrastructures and the construction of demand', PhD thesis, Lancaster University.

Chappells, H., M. Klintman, A. Linden, E. Shove, G. Spaargaren and B. Van Vliet (2000), 'Domestic Consumption, Utility Services and the Environment', final report of the Domus Project (EU DGXII – ENV-CT97-0467), Wageningen University, Wageningen.

Clark, W. (2001), 'The California challenge: energy and the environmental consequences for public utilities', *Utilities Policy*, **10**, 57–61.

Cohen, M. and J. Murphy (eds) (2001), *Exploring Sustainable Consumption: Environmental Policy and the Social Sciences,* Amsterdam: Pergamon.

Cohen, R. (1997), *Global Diasporas*, London: UCL Press.

CREM (2000), *Domeinverkenning recreëren. Milieuanalyse recreatie en toerisme in Nederland* [Domain-exploration recreation. An environmental profile of recreation and tourism in the Netherlands], Amsterdam: CREM.

Cronenberg, M. (1998), 'Das neue Energiewirtschaftsrecht' [New energy management legislation], *Recht der Energiewirtschaf,* **3**, 85–128.

Cross, G. (1993), *Time and Money: The Making of Consumer Culture,* London: Routledge.

Daly, H. (1996), *Beyond Growth: The Economics of Sustainable Development*, Boston, MA: Beacon Press.

Dean, M. (1999), *Governmentality*, London: Sage.

DEFRA (2003), *Towards Sustainable Products: A Contribution to the UK Government Strategy on Sustainable Consumption and Production*, Advisory Committee on Consumer Products and the Environment, London: HMSO.

DEMOS (1995), *The Time Squeeze*, London: Demos.

DETR (1998a), *Sustainable Development: Opportunities for Change*, London: HMSO, also available at: www.sustainable-development.gov.un/sustainable/consult1/sd007.htm, 13 August 2003.

DETR (1998b), *A New Deal For Transport*, London: Department of the Environment, Transport and the Regions.

Doyle, J. and M. Nathan (2001), *Wherever Next? Work in a Mobile World*, London: Industrial Society.

DTLR (2001), *Focus on Personal Travel*, London: DTLR/Stationery Office.

Dunn, S. (2000), *Micropower: The Next Electrical Era*, Worldwatch paper 151, Washington, DC: Worldwatch Institute.

Ekins, P. (2003), 'Environment and human behaviour: a new opportunities programme', available at: www.psi.org.uk/ehb/, 13 August.

Elias, N. (1971), *Wat is sociologie?* Aula pocket, 462, Utrecht: Het Spectrun N.V.

Elias, N. and J. Scotson (1965), *The Established and the Outsiders: A Sociological Enquiry into Community Problems*, London: Frank Cass & Co.

Elkins, P. (1991), 'The sustainable consumer society: a contradiction in terms?', *International Environmental Affairs*, Fall.

Evans, P. and T. Wurstler (2000), *Blown to Bits: How the New Economics of Information Transforms Strategy*, Boston, MA: Harvard Business School Press.

Featherstone, M. (1983), 'Consumer culture: an introduction', *Theory, Culture and Society*, **1** (3), 4–9.

Featherstone, M. (1991a), *Consumer Culture and Postmodernism*, London: Sage.

Featherstone, M. (ed.) (1991b), *The Body: Social Process and Cultural Theory*, London: Sage.

Featherstone, M. (1995), *Undoing Culture: Globalization, Postmodernism, and Identity*, London: Sage.

Fine, B. and E. Leopold (1993), *The World of Consumption*, London: Routledge.

Firestone, D. and R. Pérez-Peña (2003), 'Power failure reveals a creaky system, energy experts believe', *New York Times*, 14 August.

Fishbein, M. and I. Atzjen (1975), *Belief, Attitude, Intention and Behaviour*, Reading, MA: Addison-Wesley.

Forty, A. (1986), *Objects of Desire*, London: Thames & Hudson.

Foucault, M. (1984), *History of Sexuality 3: Care of the Self*, London: Penguin.

Foucault, M. (1997), *Ethics: The Essential Works Vol. 3*, London: Penguin.

Friedman, M. (1957), *A Theory of Consumption Function*, Princeton, NJ: Princeton University Press.

Frost, R. (1993), *Electricity in Manchester: Commemorating a Century of Electricity Supply in the City*, 1893–1993, Manchester: Neil Richardson.

GASAG (Berliner Gaswerke Gasgesellschaft) (1999), *Geschäftsbericht* [Annual Report], www.gasag.de/pdf/GASAG-GB-1999-Teil-1.pdf.

Gellings, C.W. (1996), Then and now – the perspective of the man who coined the term DSM', *Energy Policy*, **24** (4), 285–8.

Georg, S. (1999), 'The social shaping of household consumption', *Ecological Economics*, **28** (3), 455–66.

Giddens, A. (1984), *The Constitution of Society*, Cambridge: Polity Press.

Giddens, A. (1991a), *Modernity and Self-Identity*, Cambridge: Polity Press.

Giddens, A. (1991b), *The Consequences of Modernity*, Cambridge: Polity Press.

Gökalp, I. (1992), 'On the analysis of large technical systems', *Science, Technology and Human Values*, **17**, 57–78.

Goodwin, N., F. Ackerman and D. Kiron (1997), *The Consumer Society*, Washington, DC: Island Press.

Gordon, D., L. Adelman, K. Ashworth, J. Bradshaw, R. Levitas, S. Middleton, C, Pantazis, D. Patsios, S. Payne, P. Townsend and J. Williams (2000), *Poverty and Social Exclusion in Britain*, Joseph Rowntree Foundation, York: York Publishing Services.

Graham, S. (2000a), 'Introduction: cities and infrastructure networks', *International Journal of Urban and Regional Research*, **24** (1), 114–19.

Graham, S. (2000b), 'Constructing premium network spaces: reflections on infrastructure networks and contemporary urban development', *International Journal of Urban and Regional Research*, **24** (1), 183–200.

Graham, S. and S. Marvin (1994), 'Cherry picking and social dumping: utilities in the 1990s', *Utilities Policy*, **4** (2), 113–19.

Graham, S. and S. Marvin (1995), 'More than ducts and wires: post-Fordism, cities and utility networks', in P. Healey, S. Graham and S. Davoudi (eds), *Managing Cities: The New Urban Context*, London: Wiley.

Graham, S. and S. Marvin (1996), *Telecommunications and the City: Electronic Spaces, Urban Places*, London: Routledge.

Graham, S. and S. Marvin (2001), *Splintering Urbanism: Networked Infrastructures, Technological Mobilities and the Urban Condition*, London: Routledge.

Grieco, M. (1995), 'Time pressures and low income families: the implications for "social" transport policy in Europe', *Community Development Journal*, **30**, 4.

Gronow, J. and A. Warde (2001), *Ordinary Consumption*, London: Routledge.

Guy, S. and S. Marvin (1996), 'Transforming urban infrastructure provision: the emerging logic of demand side management', *Policy Studies*, **17**, 137–47.

Guy, S., S. Graham and S. Marvin (1996), 'Privatized utilities and regional governance: the new regional managers?', *Regional Studies*, **30** (8), 733–9.

Guy, S., S. Graham and S. Marvin (1997), 'Splintering networks: cities and technical networks in 1990s Britain', *Urban Studies*, **34** (2), 191–216.

Guy, S., S. Marvin and T. Moss (eds) (2001), *Urban Infrastructure in Transition: Networks, Buildings, Plans*, London: Earthscan.

Hand, M., E. Shove and D. Southerton (2003), 'Explaining daily showering: a discussion of policy and practice', ESRC Sustainable Technologies Programme Working Paper, No. 2003/4.

Hardyment, C. (1988), *From Mangle to Microwave: The Mechanization of Household Work*, Cambridge: Polity Press.

Harvey, M. (2002), 'Markets, supermarkets and the macro-social shaping of demand: an instituted economic process approach', in A. McMeekin, K. Green, M. Tomlinson and V. Walsh (eds), *Innovation by Demand:*

Interdisciplinary Approaches to the Study of Demand and its Role in Innovation, Manchester: Manchester University Press.

Herrington, P. (1996), *Climate Change and the Demand for Water*, London: HMSO.

Hewitt, P. (1993), *About Time: The Revolution in Work and Family Life*, London: Rivers Oram Press.

Hirsch, R. (1977), *The Social Limits of Growth*, London: Routledge.

Hughes, T. (1983), *Networks of Power: Electrification in Western Society, 1880–1930*, London: Johns Hopkins University Press.

Hughes, T. (1987), 'The evolution of large technological systems', in W. Bijker, T. Hughes and T. Pinch (eds), *The Social Construction of Technological Systems*, Cambridge, MA: MIT Press.

Hulme, M. and S. Peters (2001), *Me, My Phone and I: The Role of the Mobile Phone*, Lancaster: Teleconomy Group plc and Lancaster University Management School.

Hutton, W. (1998), 'Darkness at the heart of privatisation', *Observer*, 8 March.

Ilmonen, K. (2001), 'Sociology, consumption and routine', in J. Gronow and A. Warde (eds), *Ordinary Consumption*, London: Routledge.

Jacobs, M. (1995), 'Quality of life', paper from the European Science Foundation funded Lancaster workshop on Consumption, Everyday Life and Sustainability, www.comp.lancs.ac.uk/sociology/esf/qol.htm.

Juhlin, O. (1994), 'Information technology hits the automobile? Rethinking road traffic as social interaction', in J. Summerton (ed.), *Changing Large Technical Systems*, Oxford: Westview Press.

Kaul, I., I. Grünberg and M. Stern (1999), 'Defining global public goods', in I. Kaul, I. Grünberg and M. Stern, *Global Public Goods: International Cooperation in the 21st Century*, New York/Oxford: United Nations Development Programme.

Kemp, R. (1994), 'Technology and the transition to environmental sustainability; the problem of technological regime shifts', *Futures*, **26** (10), 1023–46.

Kopytoff, I. (1986), 'The cultural biography of things: commoditization as process', in A. Appadurai (ed.), *The Social Life Of Things*, Cambridge: Cambridge University Press.

Koziol, M. (2002), 'Auswirkungen des Stadtumbaus auf die kommunale Infrastruktur' [Impacts of urban restructuring on the local infrastructure], in *Stadtumbau – Wohnen und Leben mit Rückbau, Risiken, Chancen schrumpfender Städte*, Frankfurt/Oder: Institut für Stadtentwicklung und Wohnen.

Krätke, S. and R. Borst (2000), *Berlin. Metropole zwischen Boom und Krise* [Berlin. Metropolis between boom and crisis], Opladen: Leske and Budrich.

Lamont, M. (1992), *Money, Morals and Manners: The Culture of the French and American Upper-Middle Class*, London: Chicago University Press.

Latour, B. (1992), 'Where are the missing masses? The sociology of a few mundane artefacts', in W. Bijker and J. Law (eds), *Shaping Technology/Building Society*, Cambridge, MA: MIT Press.

Latour, B. (1996), *Aramis, or the Love of Technology*, Cambridge, MA: MIT Press.

Laurier, E. and C. Philo (2001), 'Meet you at junction 17: a socio-technical and spatial study of the mobile office', ESRC Award Final Report www.geog.gla.ac.uk.

Law, J. (1987), 'Technology and heterogeneous engineering: the case of Portuguese expansion', in W. Bijker, T. Hughes and T. Pinch (eds), *The Social Construction of Technological Systems: New Directions in the Sociology and History of Technology*, Cambridge, MA: MIT Press.

Levett, R., I. Christie, M. Jacobs and R. Therivel (2003), *A Better Choice of Choice: Quality of Life, Consumption and Economic Growth*, London: Fabian Society Report.

Linder, S. (1970), *The Harried Leisure Class*, New York: Columbia University Press.

Lünser, C. and A. Haeder (1998), 'Sanierung kontaminierter Standorte im Spreeknie im Südosten Berlins' [Rehabilitating contaminated sites along the Spreeknie in South-East Berlin], in *Städte mit Zukunft. Nachhaltige Stadtentwicklung in der Mitte Europas. Dokumentation*, Berlin: Senatsverwaltung für Stadtentwicklung, Umweltschutz und Technologie.

Lupton, D. (1996), *Food, the Body and the Self*, London: Sage.

Lupton, E. and J. Miller (1992), *The Bathroom, the Kitchen and the Aesthetics of Waste: A Process of Elimination*, New York: Kiosk.

Madigan, R. and M. Munro (1996), 'House beautiful: style and consumption in the home', *Sociology*, **30**, 41–57.

Marvin, S. and S. Guy (1997), 'Infrastructure provision, development processes and the co-production of environmental value', *Urban Studies*, **34** (12), 2023–6.

Marvin, S., H. Chappells and S. Guy (1999), 'Pathways of smart metering development: shaping environmental innovation', *Computers, Environment and Urban Systems*, **23** (2), 109–26.

McClintock, A. (1994), 'Soft-soaping empire: commodity racism and imperial advertising', in G. Robertson (ed.), *Travellers Tales*, London: Routledge.

McCracken, G. (1986), 'Culture and consumption: a theoretical account of the structure and movement of the cultural meaning of consumer goods', *Journal of Consumer Research*, **13**, 71–84.

McDougall, D. (2003), 'Britain in danger of blackout mayhem', *Scotsman*, 16 August.

Melosi, M. (2000), *The Sanitary City: Urban Infrastructure in America from Colonial Times to the Present*, Baltimore and London: Johns Hopkins University Press.

Menanteau, P. (1997), Energy Efficiency Labelling for Appliances: a new use of an old instrument in the French Region "Nord / Pas de Calais". *Institute of Energy Policy and Economics* (IEPE-CNRS), Paris.

Miller, D. (1987), *Material Culture and Mass Consumption*, Oxford: Blackwell.

Mol, A. (2001), *Globalization and Environmental Reform: The Ecological Modernization of the Global Economy*, Cambridge, MA: MIT Press.

Mol, A., V. Lauber and J. Liefferink (eds) (2000), *The Voluntary Approach to Environmental Policy: Joint Environmental Policy-Making in Europe*, Oxford: Oxford University Press.

Monstadt, J. (2000), *Die deutsche Energiepolitik zwischen Klimavorsorge und Liberalisierung. Räumliche Perspektiven des Wandels* [German Energy Policy between Climate Protection and Liberalization. Spatial Perspectives of the Transformation Process], Hannover: Akademie für Raumforschung und Landesplanung.

Moss, T. (2003), 'Utilities, land-use change and urban development: brownfield sites as "cold-spots" of infrastructure networks in Berlin', *Environment and Planning A*, **35** (3), 511–29.

Motivaction (1999), *Milieubelevingsgroepen in Nederland: een kwantitatief onderzoek naar drijfveren, profielen en mogelijkheden tot communicatie*, Amsterdam: Socioconsult.

National Consumer Council (1993), *Paying the Price: A Consumer View of Water, Gas, Electricity and Telephone Regulation*, London: HMSO.

National Right to Fuel Campaign and Centre for Sustainable Energy (William Baker, author) (1999), *Gas and Electricity Competition ... Who Benefits?* First Report, September.

Noorman, K. and T. Uitkerkamp (eds) (1998), *Green Households? Domestic Consumers, Environment and Sustainability*, London: Earthscan.

Norweb Distribution (1998), 'Quality of supply report', Norweb Distribution, Warrington.

Norweb Distribution (2000), 'Quality of supply report', Norweb Distribution, Warrington.

OECD (2002), *Towards Sustainable Household Consumption?: Trends and Policies in OECD Countries*, Paris: OECD.

Offner, J.M. (2000), "Territorial deregulation": local authorities at risk from technical networks', *International Journal of Urban and Regional Research*, **24** (1), 165–82.

Otnes, P. (ed.) (1988), *The Sociology of Consumption*, Oslo: Solum Forlag A/S.

Patterson, W. (2003), 'Keeping the lights on', Working Paper No. 1, Royal Institute of International Affairs, London.

Pinch, T. and W. Bijker (eds) (1987), *The Social Construction of Technological Systems*, Cambridge, MA: MIT Press.

Porter, E. (1978), *Water Management in England and Wales*, Cambridge: Cambridge University Press.

Post, M. (2000), 'Self-sufficiency: for environmental reasons or just for fun?' paper presented at the ESF Winter Workshop on Infrastructures of Consumption and the Environment, Wageningen, November.

Putnam, R. (2000), *Bowling Alone*, New York: Simon and Schuster.

Raman, S., H. Chappells, M. Klintman and B. Van Vliet (2000), *Inventory of Environmental Innovations in Domestic Utilities, the Netherlands, Britain and Sweden*, Wageningen: Wageningen University.

Redclift, M. (1996), *Wasted: Counting the Costs of Global Consumption*, London: Earthscan.

Reisch, L. (2001), 'Time and wealth: the role of time and temporalities for sustainable patterns of consumption', *Time and Society*, **10** (2/3), 387–405.

Rescon (2000), *Het project perspectief anderhalf jaar later. De stand van zaken bij 11 huishoudens* (The future perspective project a year and a half after. The state of affairs in 11 households), Utrecht: Novem.

Rose, N. (1989), *Governing the Soul: The Shaping of the Private Self*, London: Free Association Books.

Rotmans, J., R. Kemp and M. Van Asselt (2001), 'More evolution than revolution: transition management in public policy', *Foresight*, **3** (1): 16–31.

Sanne, C. (2002), 'Willing consumers – or locked-in? Policies for a sustainable consumption'. *Ecological Economics*, **42** (1–2), 273–87.

Schneider, J. (1999), *Liberalisierung der Stromwirtschaft durch regulative Marktorganisation. Eine vergleichende Untersuchung zur Reform des britischen, US-amerikanischen, europäischen und deutschen Energierechts* [Liberalizing the electricity market with regulatory market organisation. A comparative study of the reform of British, American, European and German energy legislation], Baden-Baden: Nomos.

Schor, J. (1992), *The Overworked American: The Unexpected Decline of Leisure*, London: Basic Books.

Schot, J. (1992), 'Constructive technology assessment and technology dynamics: the case of clean technologies', *Science, Technology and Human Values*, **17** (1), 36–56.

Schot, J. (1998), 'The usefulness of evolutionary models for explaining innovation: the case of the Netherlands in the nineteenth century', *History of Technology*, **14**, 173–200.

Schuttelaar & Partners (2000), *Domeinverkenning Voeden. Ingrediënten voor een gezond milieu* [Domain-exploration feeding. Ingredients for a healthy environment], Den Haag: Schuttelaar & Partners.

Schwartz-Cowan, R. (1983), *More Work for Mother: The Ironies of Household Technology from the Open Hearth to the Microwave*, London: Basic Books.

Semple, K. and J. Barron (2003), 'Parts of country may enter weekend without power', *New York Times*, 15 August.

Sennett, R. (1994), *Flesh and Stone: The Body and the City in Western Civilization*, London: Faber & Faber.

SenSUT (Senatsverwaltung für Stadtentwicklung, Umweltschutz und Technologie) (1997), *Gewerbeflächenentwicklung Berlin: Stadträumliches Konzept* [Development of commercial land in Berlin – a spatial plan], Berlin: Senatsverwaltung für Stadtentwicklung, Umweltschutz und Technologie.

SenSUT (Senatsverwaltung für Stadtentwicklung, Umweltschutz und Technologie), (1998a), *Energiebericht Berlin – Energiepolitik in Berlin 1990–1996* [Energy report for Berlin – energy policy in Berlin 1990–1996], Berlin: Senatsverwaltung für Stadtentwicklung, Umweltschutz und Technologie.

SenSUT (Senatsverwaltung für Stadtentwicklung, Umweltschutz und Technologie) (1998b), *Stadtentwicklungsplan Ver- und Entsorgung. Grundlagen* [Urban development plan for utility services. Basic principles], Berlin: Senatsverwaltung für Stadtentwicklung, Umweltschutz und Technologie.

SEU (2002), 'Making the connections: transport and social exclusion', www.cabinet-office.gov.uk/seu/publications.

Sheller, M. and J. Urry (2000), 'The city and the car', *International Journal of Urban and Regional Research*, **24**, 737–57.

Shouler, M., N. Pitts, F. Thomas and J. Hall (1997), *Water Conservation: Shower Evaluation*, BRE Report No. CR 164/97, Watford: Building Research Establishment.

Shove, E. (1997), 'Notes on comfort, cleanliness and convenience', paper for the ESF workshop on Consumption, Everyday Life and Sustainability, Lancaster, 5–8 April.

Shove, E. (1998), 'Consuming automobility', working paper prepared for SceneSusTech meeting, Bologna.

Shove, E. (2003), *Comfort, Cleanliness and Convenience: The Social Organization of Normality*, London: Berg.

Shove, E. and H. Chappells (2001), 'Ordinary consumption and extraordinary relationships: utilities and their users', in J. Gronow and A. Warde (eds), *Ordinary Consumption*, London: Routledge.

Shove, E. and D. Southerton (2000), 'Defrosting the freezer: from novelty to convenience: a story of normalization', *Journal of Material Culture*, **5** (3), 5–25.

Shove, E. and A. Warde (2002), 'Inconspicuous consumption: the sociology of consumption, lifestyles and the environment', in R. Dunlap, F. Buttel, P. Dickens and A. Gijswijt (eds), *Sociological Theory and the Environment: Classic Foundations, Contemporary Insights*, Lanham, MA: Rowman & Littlefield.

Silverstone, R. (1993), 'Time, information and communication technologies and the household', *Time and Society*, **2**, 283–311.

Siohansi, F. (2002), 'California's electricity market: finally turning the corner?', *Energy Policy*, **30** (2), 245–8.

Slater, D. (1997), *Consumer Culture and Modernity*, Cambridge: Polity.

Southerton, D. (2003), 'Squeezing time: allocating practices, co-ordinating networks and scheduling society', *Time and Society*, **12**, 5–25.

Southerton, D. and M. Tomlinson (2003), "Pressed for Time" – the differential impacts of a "time squeeze", CRIC Discussion Paper No. 60, University of Manchester and UMIST.

Spaargaren, G. (1997), *The Ecological Modernization of Production and Consumption. Essays in Environmental Sociology*, PhD Thesis, Wageningen: Wageningen University.

Spaargaren, G. (2000), 'Ecological modernization theory and domestic consumption', *Journal of Environmental Policy and Planning*, **2** (4), 323–35.

Spaargaren, G. (2001), 'Milieuverandering en het alledaagse leven' [Environmental change and everyday life], inaugural address, Tilburg, Tilburg University.

Spaargaren, G. (2003), 'Sustainable consumption: a theoretical and environmental policy perspective', *Society and Natural Resources*, **16** (8), 687–701.

Spaargaren, G., S. Martens and T. Beckers (forthcoming), 'Sustainable technologies and everyday life: social practices in transition', in A. Slob and P. Verbeek (eds), *Technology, Behaviour and the Environment*, London: Kluwer Academic Publishers.

Staats, H. and P. Harland (1995), *The Ecoteam Program in the Netherlands*, Leiden: Leiden University.

Star, S. (1999), 'The ethnography of infrastructure', *American Behavioural Scientist*, **43** (3), 377–91.

Statistisches Bundesamt (2001), *Statistisches Jahrbuch* [Statistical yearbook], Wiesbaden: Statistisches Bundesamt.

Statistisches Landesamt Berlin (1994, 1999, 2001), *Statistisches Jahrbuch* [Statistical Yearbook], Berlin: Kulturbuch-Verlag.

Stern, P., T. Dietz and G. Guagnano (1995), 'The new ecological paradigm is sociopsychological context', *Environmental Behaviour*, **27**, 723–43.

Stradling, S. (2002), 'Behavioural research in road safety: tenth seminar', www.dft.gov.uk/stellent/groups/dft_rdsafety/documents/pdf/dft_rdsafety_pdf_504575.pdf.

Strasser, S. (1999), *Waste and Want: A Social History of Trash*, New York: Metropolitan Books.

Summerton, J. (1994), 'Introductory essay: the systems approach to technological change', in J. Summerton (ed.), *Changing Large Technical Systems*, Oxford: Westview Press.

Summerton, J. (2000), 'Out of anonymity: shaping new identities for electrons, utilities and consumers in Swedish electricity in the 1990s', contribution to the winter workshop on Infrastructures of Consumption and the Environment, Wageningen, November.

Summerton, J. (2002), 'Do electrons have politics? Constructing user identities in Swedish electricity', forthcoming in *Science, Technology & Human Values*, 2004.

Swann, P. (2002), 'There's more to the economics of consumption than (almost) unconstrained utility maximisation', in A. McMeekin, K. Green, M. Tomlinson and V. Walsh (eds), *Innovation by Demand: An Interdisciplinary Approach to the Study of Demand and its Role in Innovation*, Manchester: Manchester University Press.

Swedish Consumer Authority (2000), *Tjänste bra? Marknad, kvalitet och klagomål – konsumenter om nio tjänstebranscher*, Stockholm, RRV 2000:20.

Swedish Consumer Authority (2002), *Konsekvenser för konsumenter av nyligen konkurrensutsatta marknader – elmarknaden*, Stockholm, Regeringsrapport December.

Swedish National Audit Office (2000), *Kunden är lös! – konsumenternas agerande på de omreglerade el- och telemarknaderna*, Stockholm, RRV 2000:20.

Swedish National Audit Office (2001) *Att skapa aktiva konsumenter: Energimyndighetens och Konsumentverkets stöd till konsumenterna på elmarknaden*, Stockholm: RRV 2001:10.

Swedish National Energy Administration (2002), *Handelsmarginaler och förutsättningar inom elhandel – Energimyndighetens slutsatser*, Dnr 00-02-205, Stockholm, 31 October.

Thøgersen, J. and F. Ölander (2001), 'Spillover of environment-friendly consumer behaviour', paper for the 5th Nordic Environmental Research Conference, Aarhus, 14–16 June.

TNO (1999), *Duurzame consumptie: Verkenning Kleding* [Sustainable consumption: domain-exploration clothing], Delft: TNO/STB.

Truffer, B., J. Voss and K. Konrad (2002), 'Integrated microsystems of supply, anticipation, evaluation and shaping of transformation in the German utility sector', paper for the EASST Responsibility under Uncertainty Conference, 31 July–2 August, York.

Turton, P. (1998), 'The UK Experience', presentation at CIWEM Water Conservation and Re-use Seminar, February, CIWEM.

Urry, J. (2000), *Sociology Beyond Societies*, London: Routledge.

Urry, J. (2002), 'Mobility and proximity', *Sociology*, **36**, 255–74.

Urry, J. (2003a), 'Social networks, travel and talk', *British Journal of Sociology*, **54**, 155–75.

Urry, J. (2003b), *Global Complexity*, Cambridge: Polity.

Van Mierlo, B. (1997), *De totstandkoming van twee grote Pilotprojecten met zonnecellen in nieuwbouwwijken. Een vergelijking tussen Amsterdam en Amersfoort*, Amsterdam: IVAM.

Van Vliet, B. (2002), *Greening the Grid: The Ecological Modernisation of Network-Bound Systems*, PhD Thesis, Wageningen: Wageningen University.

Van Vliet, B. (2003), 'Differentiation and ecological modernisation in water and electricity provision and consumption', *Innovation*, **16** (1), 29–49.

Van Vliet, B., R. Wüstenhagen and H. Chappells (2000), 'New provider–consumer relations in electricity provision. Green electricity schemes in the UK, the Netherlands, Switzerland and Germany', paper for the Business Strategy and the Environment Conference, 18–19 September, Leeds.

Veblen, T. (1998), *The Theory of the Leisure Class: An Economic Study of Institutions*, London: Allen & Unwin [first published 1899].

Vigar, G. (2002), *The Politics of Mobility*, London: Spon.

Vigarello, G. (1988), *Concepts of Cleanliness: Changing Attitudes in France Since the Middle Ages*, Cambridge: Cambridge University Press.

Von Meier, A. (1994), 'Integrating supply technologies into utility power systems: possibilities for reconfiguration', in J. Summerton (ed.), *Changing Large Technical Systems*, Oxford: Westview Press.

Von Weizsäcker, E., A. Lovins and L. Lovins (1998), *Factor Four: Doubling Wealth – Halving Resource Use*, London: Earthscan.

Vringer, K. and K. Blok (1993), *The Direct and Indirect Energy Requirement of Households in the Netherlands*, Utrecht: Vakgroep Natuurwetenschap en Samenleving.

VROM (2000), *De warme golfstroom: heroriëntatie op communicatie over milieu* [The warm gulf-stream: reconsidering environmental communication], Den Haag: Centrale Directie Communicatie DGM.

Wackernagel, M. and W. Rees (1995), *Our Ecological Footprint*, Gabriola Island, BC: New Society Publishers.

Warde, A. (1990), 'Introduction to the sociology of consumption', *Sociology*, **24** (1), 1–4.

Warde, A. (1999), 'Convenience food: space and timing', *British Food Journal*, **101** (7), 518–27.

Webb, P. and S. Suggitt (2000), *Gadgets and Necessities: An Encyclopedia of Household Innovations*, London: ABC-CLIO.

Whitelegg, J. (1997), *Critical Mass*, London: Pluto.

Wight, D. (1993), *Workers not Wasters*, Edinburgh: Edinburgh University Press.

Wilhite, H. (1997), 'Cultural aspects of consumption', paper for the ESF workshop on Consumption, Everyday Life and Sustainability, Lancaster, 5–8 April.

Winsemius, P. (1986), *Gast in eigen huis: Beschouwingen over milieumanagement*, Alphen aan de Rijn: Samsom.

Wright, L. (1960), *Clean and Decent*, London: Penguin.

Zeeman, G. and G. Lettinga (1999), 'The role of anaerobic digestion of domestic sewage in closing the water and nutrient cycle at community level', *Water Science and Technology*, **39**, 187–94.

Zerubavel, E. (1979), *Hidden Rhythms: Patterns of Time in Hospital Life*, Chicago, IL: Chicago University Press.

Index